Received on

ıry

NO LONGER PROPERTY
SEATTLE PUBLIC LIBRARY

My (Part-Time) Paris Life

My (Part-Time) Paris Life

....

How Running
Away Brought Me Home

Lisa Anselmo

Thomas Dunne Books
St. Martin's Press 〽 *New York*

THOMAS DUNNE BOOKS.

An imprint of St. Martin's Press.

MY (PART-TIME) PARIS LIFE. Copyright © 2016 by Lisa Anselmo. All rights reserved. Printed in the United States of America. For information, address St. Martin's Press, 175 Fifth Avenue, New York, N.Y. 10010.

www.thomasdunnebooks.com

www.stmartins.com

Library of Congress Cataloging-in-Publication Data

Names: Anselmo, Lisa, author.
Title: My (part-time) Paris life : how running away brought me home / Lisa Anselmo.
Description: First edition. | New York : Thomas Dunne Books/ St. Martin's Press, 2016.
Identifiers: LCCN 2016007864| ISBN 9781250067470 (hardcover) | ISBN 9781466875821 (e-book)
Subjects: LCSH: Anselmo, Lisa. | Anselmo, Lisa—Homes and haunts— France—Paris. | Paris (France)—Biography. | Paris (France)— Desctription and travel. | Paris (France)—Social life and customs. | Women—France—Paris—Biography. | Americans—France— Paris—Biography. | Self-actualization (Psychology) | Mothers and daughters—United States. | Mothers—United States—Death. | BISAC: BIOGRAPHY & AUTOBIOGRAPHY / Personal Memoirs. | TRAVEL / Europe / France.
Classification: LCC DC705.A57 A3 2016 | DDC 944/ .361084092—dc23
LC record available at https://lccn.loc.gov/2016007864

Our books may be purchased in bulk for promotional, educational, or business use. Please contact your local bookseller or the Macmillan Corporate and Premium Sales Department at 1-800-221-7945, extension 5442, or by e-mail at MacmillanSpecialMarkets @macmillan.com.

First Edition: October 2016

10   9   8   7   6   5   4   3   2   1

For Ma

Paris . . . too real and too beautiful.
It reaches in and opens you wide, and you stay that way.

—*An American in Paris*

My (Part-Time)
Paris Life

Café L'Ingénu, 11th Arrondissement, Paris

Who do you think you are?

This probably stops more people from doing more things than any other question. Who are you to want more? You think you deserve it? Really?

People say that greatness is inspiring, but what they really mean is only as long as it's someone else's greatness, someone who lives on another plane, someone they saw portrayed in a film. Like Gandhi.

But greatness close up? In themselves? In *you*? Terrifying.

Crabs in a bucket, a friend once called it. Just try to break out, shoot for more, and those around you will grab ahold and tug you back to "reality." Who do you think *you* are? Are you better than *us*?

Maybe it's envy—or fear of being shown there's a better way. Because once you know there's a better way, and you don't follow it, life in the bottom of that bucket becomes unbearable.

And who wants that? Better to stay where you are, where the misery is warm and familiar. Where you can tell yourself it's good enough, and you should be lucky to have what you have.

My mother wanted more for herself. As a young girl she dreamed of being an artist. She had talent, too. When she was about ten years old, she saw an advertisement, once ubiquitous in magazines, featuring a drawing of a pirate or a turtle, with the headline "Draw Me—Win a 2-Year Art Scholarship!" You drew your best copy of the character and sent it in. Then you "won" enrollment in an art school, along with art supplies, for which you received a bill. Of course, my mother was too young to understand; her passion drove her to take that chance, possibly the boldest in her life. Her parents did what any Depression-era immigrants would have done: they freaked out. My grandfather had to hire a lawyer with his meager mason's income to get my mother out of the contract. That was the end of her dream, then and there.

When I was around the same age as my mother when she drew that pirate, I did nearly the same thing. My dream was to be a writer, so I sent my novel, all one hundred fourteen handwritten pages of it, to a publisher whose ad I saw in *Tiger Beat* magazine. Upon reviewing my masterwork, the publisher sent me a letter saying they'd love to publish me—and would I please send a certified check for one hundred fifty dollars? My parents opened this letter before I did, after which they sat me down and gave me a lecture on taking risks that wasn't as inspirational as I think they imagined it was: they told me if I was serious they'd help me find a proper publisher, but something in their demeanor said, *Whoa! You stop that!* I wouldn't take writing seriously again for decades.

Who do you think you are?

The crabs-in-a-bucket thinking is passed down. Though I'd done exactly as my mother had, she couldn't do anything but what her parents had taught her, and pulled me back from that scary unknown, keeping me safely tucked away with her.

We see greatness as foreign, intimidating; we even shame it out of people, out of ourselves. We're taught that humility is the noblest quality, but we confuse humility with shrinking away from the world. Even Gandhi led a nation while being humble.

Being your fullest self, putting yourself out into the world with arms and eyes wide—that's the greatness I'm talking about. Knowing you deserve to be happy.

My mother didn't know she deserved happiness, and she passed that on to her children. No matter how great she told us we were, we learned more from watching how she treated herself. It's not really what other people say, is it? It always comes down to "Mirror, mirror on the wall . . ."

Maybe it's finally leaving that dead-end job, extracting yourself from a bad marriage, starting your own business—whatever it is, there's a point when you realize you can't keep living this way: your head spins all day, you don't sleep anymore, you can't shake an overwhelming sense of dread. The only thing that keeps you going is the dream of something better, something more. You fixate on that, and it helps you wade through whatever muck you're mired in. You tell yourself, *one day*. One day you'll make that move, and your life will begin for real.

But you're waiting. Waiting for that moment when everything will line up, when you'll feel stronger, when you'll have more money. When you'll be really ready to make a change.

Except, I'm here to tell you that moment is never coming.

You're not waiting to be ready; you're waiting for someone to give you permission. Forget about it. Just start clawing your way out of that bucket.

I got out, eventually—when I was so deep down and buried in the dark and had only up to go. After I clawed my way out, I fell into Paris.

That's when everything changed.

PART 1

. . . .

Is There Life After Death?

One

Hope Will Out

My mother was the most beautiful woman in the world. She was Audrey Hepburn thin, chic, and classy, always put together with her ever-present red lipstick. I pitied all the other kids because their mothers were not my mother. Ma was perfect in every way.

At least I thought so until I was four.

I was watching her put on her makeup one morning, something I loved doing, especially when she brushed on her liquid eyeliner with one sweeping motion, a delicate swoop at the outer corner of each eye. She was glorious; she was a princess.

"Ugly," she said to her reflection in the mirror.

That word flipped my entire world on its edge, sending everything I believed flying. My mind scrambled to gather it up again, to make sense of it. If Ma was ugly, then what was I? If Ma wasn't perfect and beautiful, then what was?

That was the day I learned about worthlessness.

Even before that day, I sensed Ma wasn't happy deep down. Not that I was fully aware of it, being so young, but I could feel something in the air that unsettled me.

Ma hadn't wanted to move to that one-horse town in New Jersey, away from our whole family in Buffalo, New York, a thriving metropolis of two million people. But Dad got transferred, so off we went. I was two and a half, but I still remember her tears.

Those first few years were the hardest; we knew no one in New Jersey, and with my father at work and my older sister, Maria, in school, it was just my mother and I most of the day. I remember tea parties with chocolate milk and peanut butter finger sandwiches—and the weight of my mother's loneliness.

She used to say I was attached to her hip, but I wonder who needed whom more.

The day I went off to kindergarten, Ma cried all the way to the bus stop. That day, I learned that going out into the world was a scary thing. This was no way to inspire her little chick to fly, but that was Ma. She didn't know who she was without her children.

I was a fearful, clingy child. Maybe Ma made me that way, and maybe I was just sensitive and artistic like her. I spent a lot of time in my room reading, writing, dreaming. I didn't understand other children very well—even as a child, I thought them childish. I suppose I spent too much time with Ma. I adored her, hung on her every word—her every mood.

But then, we all did. Ma's moods set the tone of the day for all of us. When she was happy, it was heaven. She doted on her children—played with us, read to us. She had a tremendous sense of humor, could be giddy and silly, suddenly bursting into song, grabbing one of us for a jitterbug in the kitchen. We'd wail and roll our eyes, "Maaaaa, stop it!"

In truth, you didn't want it to stop, because when the mood shifted, it could be devastating, mostly because it seemed to come out of nowhere. One minute we'd be doing homework, and the next, Ma would be screaming at us about having six inches of dust in our rooms. The dust, the dust! Something had set her off, something we couldn't understand.

The heartbreak wasn't that she was screaming at us; it was that she'd been happy and wasn't anymore—and now, neither were we. I wanted to make the ugly beautiful again.

In our early years, we often existed in the space between Ma's moods, waiting for the other shoe to drop. I started to believe I could make it better; fixing my mother's pain was how I coped with the instability of our lives. I learned to please, to overachieve, to be a source of pride. My strategy was simple: don't piss off Ma.

She could be strict, rigid sometimes. Critical. It's how she was raised and how she raised us. I learned to work within the rules of the house, work around them. Maria coped another way: she kept stirring things up.

Maria fought our mother on everything, threw violent tantrums, seemingly thriving on the chaos she created. By the time Maria was a teenager, the screaming matches between her and Ma were the new mood killers around the house.

The further my sister pulled away, the harder Ma tugged me close. I could feel her pain—Dad's, too, and that only made me paddle faster to keep things from sinking. I was the good daughter, the one who got straight As, the one who did her chores, soloed in the chorus. I felt important and useful—and in control. Somewhere in there I convinced myself I was the one holding it together.

Someone had to, right?

I grew to resent my sister, my parents' helplessness, but felt guilty about it because I loved them, too. A familiar mix of emotions. My way of dealing with Maria's pain was the same as it had been with my mother's: assuage it any way I could. Keep things calm. Mediate. Moderate.

Or hole up in my room. There was always that.

I couldn't understand why Maria was so intent on screwing everything up. Why fight? Wouldn't it be easier just to go along with the status quo? Like I did?

But that wasn't her role in our family. She was the bludgeon, shattering the delicate order of things as Ma had done, and I was the broom, furiously sweeping up after them.

The damage was done. Ma's sense of worthlessness had seeped into both of us. I compensated with perfectionism; Maria with rebellion. Whatever the tactic, both of us kept ourselves from taking part—from taking risks.

I remained the responsible one, the good daughter, the fixer, way into adulthood—long after it was needed for survival. It was hardwired into me now. My sister moved away to Florida, while I stayed close by, in New York, and naturally became Ma's go-to girl, especially after Dad died.

Ma slotted me into his role as companion and problem solver, a role perfectly suited to me, one that was created all those years ago when we first moved to New Jersey. Once again, we were attached at the hip.

I'd visit her on weekends and we'd go antiquing, or have high tea at a café in the neighboring town, one of those quaint villages that boasted, GEORGE WASHINGTON SLEPT HERE. Or we'd just sit in her kitchen for hours, yakking away. We never ran out of things to talk about, the two of us so alike we were more sisters than mother and daughter.

Our relationship had grown up, and I had the best of Ma now, the happy Ma. We had each other.

Thanksgiving and Easter were just Ma and me. Mother's Day, too. And Ma's birthday. We created our own holiday traditions for the two of us—Thanksgiving in New York at a swanky restaurant; Easter at her house, where we dyed eggs together for our Sunday breakfast. I'd still find the token chocolate bunny beside my plate, no matter how old I was. Maybe our relationship hadn't quite grown up all the way.

I helped Ma decorate for Christmas, prepare her taxes, plant her garden. She always rewarded me with my favorite roasted chicken with crispy potatoes. Her reliance on me grew as she aged, but for all my complaints about wanting a life of my own, I needed her as much as she needed me. I liked my role as fixer daughter; it made me feel important. And as long as there was Ma, I could exist safely inside the boundaries of her needs and expectations, my responsibilities keeping me from venturing too far from the safe and familiar.

The problem with making your mother your best friend is that, well, your mother is your best friend. The shrinks have a word for that: *codependence*.

When we got the news that Ma's breast cancer had come back after fifteen years in remission, it was already stage three. By the time we were decorating her house for Christmas, it was stage four.

After six weeks, a hospital becomes less horrible, especially when you have someone you love in one of the beds. It's surprising how fast you bond with the place. When you're in a hospital day after day, you become deeply attached to the people who work there, because each of them is a sign of hope, a line tossed over the side of the rescue vessel. You cling for dear life.

Routine is critical when you're a daily hospital visitor. Anything to make it seem normal. As you pass through those familiar front doors each day, you no longer recoil from the smell—a potpourri of floor polish, antiseptic, and bodily fluids. You wave to the guard at the entrance. *Hello, dude I see every day.* That's your guy, your "welcome back" guy. The guy who helped you get a taxi when you were hysterical. And you swear that, after the third week of seeing you, pity is starting to show in his eyes.

By now, you're on a first-name basis with the volunteers at the gift shop, the cashier at the cafeteria. You've developed a personal relationship with the entire staff—nurses, assistants, interns, specialists. Particularly the nurses and assistants. They're the ones who are really doing all the work. A good one can make your day; a great one can save the day. You know their schedules. You bake treats for the nurses' station—because that's what the regulars do, especially when gratitude kicks in. When it's your mother, you don't want someone just going through the motions, tuning out when your mother cries all night because the morphine is making her hallucinate. You want that person on the floor to remember your face, your tears, your thank-yous—to see a mother with a loving family, not the cancer patient in Room 301, Bed 1.

It's survival in a place of survival.

You feel yourself pulling apart, but you hold it together with everything you have. When your mother needs you, you muster courage and strength from somewhere deep. It's the only way, because a hospital forces you to make decisions no person in your state of mind should ever have to make, like, do you want to sign a DNR—a "Do Not Resuscitate" order. Meaning, if your mother should go into cardiac arrest, the hospital should not save her. They should just let her die.

They send in a young doctor, one who looks like he drew the short straw, to explain gently—so, so gently—that in your mother's weakened state and advanced years, the chest compressions needed to start her heart again would shatter her ribs, and, well, she's already had to undergo hip surgery because she fell in the rehab facility just when things were looking up. Now she's on a downward spiral and probably can't be brought back. The doctor asks the patient's beleaguered daughters, who are on the brink of exhaustion, if they really want to put their mother through any further aggressive, lifesaving treatment at this point.

You blink.

Ma's dying?

The man waits for your response with eyes big and round, a pen in his hand.

Jesus, Ma's dying.

So? Do you want your mother's ribs crushed while they're trying to save her for what might be only one more day?

No, of course you don't. In theory.

The man reminds you that your mother had a living will, as if this will make it easier. You're simply doing what she wanted. If you want to, of course; it's not for them to tell you what to do. Except the DNR the man is holding is already filled out. All it needs is your signature.

You ask for the pen. You watch your hand sign your name.

Then you throw up in the john.

Our mother's decline was so swift it threw us into a perpetual grasping state, hurtling downhill with her, desperate to catch her before she hit the bottom and broke our world apart.

No one grasped harder than I, frantically managing our mother's care, liaising between her oncologist, cardiologist, urologist, nephrologist, generalist. If I pushed hard enough, spun fast enough, I could save her. I *needed* to save her. She was everything.

Then she was gone.

Suddenly, I had only myself to worry about. The first words out of my mouth when my mother's last breath left hers: "Oh my God, now what?"

There was a great big hole where my life should have been.

Some people say the first year after a death is the hardest. I don't agree. In that first year after Ma died, I was still numb. That's why I could plan a memorial concert and organize a team for a breast cancer walk on Ma's birthday. Why my sister and I could go to Paris for Christmas and have a beautiful time—in every photo, toasting our mother with wistful, poetic smiles of those who can only be numb. In the first year, we were swaddled in the love and sympathy of family and friends, like a morphine drip keeping the pain dull and our heads hazy.

Then the second year rolled around, and Ma was still dead.

The friends had gone back to their lives; the sympathy at work had dried up. When I received the "We really need you to show up on time" speech, I knew the honeymoon was over. But I was just starting to feel the pain. It took a year after the wound was made, but there the pain finally was, sharp and relentless.

My dining table was piled high with Ma's estate papers, thousands of dollars in medical bills, stacks of her mail, now diverted to me, needing to be canceled. According to the U.S. Postal Service and direct mail databases, my mother was still alive. Her beloved charities, her favorite catalogues—fragments of her daily life—arrived in my mailbox every day. Every piece of mail like a punch in the gut: *Ma's life is no more.* Selfish marketing bastards trying to sell stuff to a dead woman.

An endless deluge of mail, of pain, came in—so much that I had to carve out an hour every day to call or email these organizations and notify them of Ma's death. Some would reply and express their shock and sadness, especially the smaller charities she'd helped keep afloat. I began every day like this, breaking bad news, ending Ma's relationships. *Deceased* was a word I wrote hundreds of times. "Please remove her from your database, she is deceased." *Remove her.* The one person who wanted her alive was actually helping to delete her from existence.

I still had to function; I was an executive creative director in a large publishing company, yet getting myself out of bed was becoming more difficult each day. When I didn't have to go to work, I'd sleep until one in the afternoon, get out of bed around four. Laundry piled up. So did the dishes in the sink, the dust.

What was the point? Death was inevitable, wasn't it?

My mother was eighty-three when she died. People would always say, "Well, she lived a good, long life," presumably to comfort me. But Ma didn't want to die; she wasn't ready to die. There were a couple of rough nights in hospice toward the end, when we'd get a call saying she was dying. We'd rush over there, but she'd hang on. She was anxious, would call out. We couldn't calm her. She'd fight sleep as if it were the Reaper. She would shout at her dead sister, "Helen! Helen! Go away!" If her sister was coming to take her, well, she wasn't going—no effing way.

There was still so much to do.

I know she had regrets, dreams unfulfilled. The end came too soon, as far as she was concerned. To say "She lived a good, long life" was an insult to her, and to her children—a pat dismissal of the magnitude of our grief.

Watching Ma fighting death, I felt more fragile. After she died, it grew more intense, this fragility. I hung on to my own life with the same tragic tenacity. So much to do. Would I get to do it, or would I die with a long, unchecked list of regrets? It's all I could think about: Would I matter? Would my life have been for anything in the end? Everything seemed futile, and tragic.

Around this time, I convinced myself that the Mayan end-of-the-world myth was true. It wasn't a conscious thought, but it worked on me in the background. I started to stash money around the house. I bought six gallons of water and canned goods, a seven-hour backup battery. I would survey my possessions regularly and agonize over what I would take if I had to flee—you know, to catch that end-of-the-world evacuation bus. I understood without a doubt we were going to die, and it seemed as if I was the only one who knew, or cared, which only made it worse.

Or, with my luck, I'd be a survivor and would have to bear witness to the carnage, this Mayan doom. I didn't want to be a survivor. If the end was coming, I wanted to be right in Times Square with a target on my chest. In fact, screw it—maybe I'd just beat the Mayans to it. Why suffer longer than I had to? It was just a matter of how to do it and finding the will to do it.

A moment of courage, and I'd be free from the pain.

But the mind is an amazing thing. As long as you keep breathing, it keeps you wanting to breathe. And my mind began to fixate on a tiny dot of light, a pinpoint of hope in the form of an apartment in Paris. That hopeful part of my mind that wanted to live went online and looked at apartments for sale in the City of Light.

That first day, I looked at a few places. Then a few more. Suddenly, it was two o'clock in the morning.

The next day, I didn't have to psych myself up just to coax a leg over the side of the bed. I jumped up and went back online. I looked at a few more apartments. Eight hours passed.

Four weeks. Six weeks. Two hours after work each night and entire weekends searching, exploring: million-dollar mansions in Saint-Germain-des-Prés, small attic studios in Montmartre. Every dream was indulged. My mind was on a mission.

The obsession became organized into folders: by neighborhood, by size, by price per square meter. I wasn't really going to buy anything, but it didn't matter.

The dot of light, of hope, started to expand.

· Two ·

Paris Was an Accident

I hated Paris.

I was sixteen, and my French class took a trip over Easter break. Paris was the last stop on a multicity tour of Switzerland and France—thirteen high school kids from northern New Jersey transported to Europe, where we'd practice our French and soak up some culture.

It was a big deal for our little town, and a reporter from the local paper was on hand for our departure. They posed us as hitchhikers for the photo, me thumbing a ride, and my friends Dawn and Karin holding a handmade sign that read, PARIS 7000 KM. The sign maker was off by a couple thousand kilometers, but it didn't seem to matter. That Paris was somewhere far away was the point.

The trip cost eight hundred dollars—steep for my parents at the time, but Ma insisted I go even if we had to eat polenta three nights a week for six months to save the money. *Someone* from our family would see Europe.

Whoever made Switzerland first on the agenda knew what he was doing. It was the perfect ambassador for Europe: immaculate, manicured, sleepy, with gentle and impossibly polite citizens. Half-timbered buildings lined the streets, their window boxes stuffed with tulips. It was like Disney's Swiss World—too perfect to be real.

The Alps, crowned in white, presided over all, their hillsides dotted with wee wooden chalets that looked exactly like a music box my aunt Mary had, the one in the parlor by the stairs—coveted by her niece, who was prone to dreaming of faraway places. If you lifted the roof of one of those Alpine chalets, would you find a miniature lady turning slowly to the tune "Edelweiss"?

The highlights of Switzerland for a bunch of kids: peeling bubbly, chewy cheese crust from the bottom of the fondue pot; eating so much creamy milk chocolate that we were rolling on the floor giggling, happily hopped up on sugar.

One morning at breakfast, I ordered a hot cocoa, and the waiter brought a cup of steamed milk with a foil pouch set on the saucer. The steamed milk was sexy enough, but what shook out of that pouch was not the usual sandy concoction. Those magical, wonderful Swiss used *real chocolate shavings*. The shavings surrendered to the hot milk, transforming it into liquid pudding. Everyone at our breakfast table leaned in with wide eyes and gaping mouths. This must be what they meant by haute cuisine.

I'm sure we saw some sights; I remember our tour bus stopping in front of a bear in Berne so we could take a photo, but for me, that cup of decadent liquid pudding was the best part of Europe. I was moving here and drinking that hot chocolate every single day. I was utterly in love.

Then we landed in Paris.

In the early 1980s, a shroud of filth clung to the buildings there. The gutters smelled of sewage; you couldn't drink the water. The toilet paper was brown and the consistency of packing tissue. My mother, knowing this, had tucked a roll of Scott into my carry-on, making me the most popular girl in the tour group as I doled out squares like an acid dealer in Washington Square Park.

And the Parisians? Brusque, sharp, angry. Maybe it was the toilet paper—who could say?—but they were a far cry from the Swiss. The women's faces were tight and scowling; the men leered at us. We were kicked around like dogs underfoot, while they sighed and rolled their eyes. At one point, a homeless man whipped an object at my friend's face; it looked like a sock stuffed with something. "Go home, American," he said. It wasn't a sock. Dangling from his hand by its tail: a dead rat.

Yeah, Paris was swell.

The hotel we stayed in, called, quite unfortunately for the country, Hôtel de France, was on rue de Lyon, in the shadow of the Lyon train station, a place surrounded by sex shops and prostitutes. The narrow six-story structure looked as if it were being propped up by the buildings on either side. Frozen in 1890, the faded oak-paneled lobby had a rickety cage elevator strung up inside a curving staircase. Tattered Persian-esque carpeting ran up the stairs; crazed and yellowing paint covered the walls. But I suppose when your clients just pop in for a quickie with the local tradeswomen, you don't bother to invest in upkeep. Most of the rooms didn't even have toilets, just a shower stall in one corner.

The maids wore paper shower caps and blue lab coats, as if cleaning the rooms were an industrial job. Maybe they just hosed the place down with disinfectant between guests.

Our room sagged like a weary old woman. The century-old furniture, once beautiful, begged to be put out of its misery. One of the doors of the armoire hung precariously on one remaining hinge. A small breakfast table wobbled when I put my purse on it; I quickly snatched it off again. Would they jail you in France if you broke their furniture?

The bed sighed when I sat on it, and when I stood again, a deep imprint remained. The bed linens were made from what looked like old flour sacks. The next day, we would wake with elbows raw and red. Maybe this was why the Parisians were so angry.

The room did have two things going for it: a view of the Eiffel Tower and an en suite bathroom equipped with the only bathtub in the entire hotel. Large and deep, it had a gold-plated fixture on which hung a handheld showerhead like the receiver on a phone. Porcelain inlays read, CHAUD and FROID.

In fact, we seemed to be overstocked in bathtubs. We even had a baby bath—at least that's what we figured it was used for. It was in its own stall in the corner of the room, separate from the main bathroom. When I turned on the faucet, water shot up from a sprayer in the middle of the basin, splattering the ceiling and soaking us. Our screams echoed in the courtyard of the hotel.

The French were seriously weird.

We saw Paris from the windows of a tour bus, shown the sights at a dizzying pace, everything blending together. I snapped pictures just to catalogue the event, because I thought I should. Who knew, maybe it was something important I'd care about later. But I was detached. I missed my chocolate-covered land of chalets, and begrudged Paris. I was tired; I wanted to go home.

That might have been the end of Paris and me, but our French teacher had other ideas.

There are a few moments that, even as you live them, you know will stay with you forever: the ones that shape you. One of those moments for me came halfway through our third day, when our small group ditched the tour bus and went around on its own. It was a Friday; the sky was flawless; the air smelled of flowering trees with just a dash of diesel.

Wherever we went, we went on foot and could move among the Parisians, hear their conversations, make eye contact. We visited our teacher's favorite places, such as the Latin Quarter, with its narrow cobbled streets, cool and quiet, where the rest of the city fell away. In the Tuileries, we sat on dainty green folding chairs and ate sandwiches as the sun baked into us. We bought sheet music on rue de Rome; drank Cokes in a belle epoque café under a soaring trompe l'oeil ceiling. And that night, we went to Montmartre.

If I was still on the fence about Paris by that point, Montmartre gave me the nudge I needed. A hilltop village high above the city, it reminded me of Switzerland, with its winding lanes and quaint cottages. The district pulsed with vibrant energy, hummed with live music. We walked along rue des Abbesses, past cafés filled with diners; rode the funicular up to the Sacré-Coeur Basilica and looked out over the city twinkling below.

I was too young to be jaded by the quarter's touristy trappings. I saw only the café life, the young students—and the pretty man drawing portraits in Place du Tertre for thirty francs a pop. With wavy auburn hair, a thick red beard, and a cable-knit sweater like a young Hemingway, he flirted with us in lightly accented English as he drew our likenesses.

Paris began its courtship with me, but I wouldn't fall in love until two decades later.

In the late nineties, I was mad for Italy. Everyone was. We'd all come down with Tuscan fever—the décor, food, popular literature. Italy, for an Italian American like me, was the ultimate validation. I was dreaming up a future there, had a ten-year plan. Sooner, if I met a nice Italian boy.

I'd been going there every year; it was dirt cheap before the euro kicked in. By 2001, Italy was becoming like another home. Then September 11 happened. I lost my job, and the dollar hit the skids. Italy, and happiness, was on hold.

Early the next year, a friend asked me to join her in Paris for her birthday. I wasn't so keen. Wouldn't she rather go to Rome or Florence? But no, she was in love with the City of Light for some reason, probably because no one had thrown a rat in her face.

I was working only part-time and would need convincing to spend the money. That conversation went like this:

She: There's a special. Round-trip airfare is three hundred thirty-five dollars.
Me: Huh.
She: Room with a view of the Eiffel Tower. I'm staying on points, so it's free.
Me: Oh?

She: And access to the Executive Lounge. Free drinks.
Me: When do we leave?

All I'd need, beyond the cheap airfare, was some spending money. Who could say no to Europe for five hundred dollars? And free drinks? So, I lined my carry-on with a dozen tissue packs in lieu of a roll of Scott, and off to Paris I went.

What a difference twenty years makes.

Gone was the filth I'd remembered: the gutters seemed *spotless*, the buildings glistened white in the sun. The city was impossibly, dazzlingly beautiful everywhere I looked.

It turned out I didn't need my tissues; the French had made huge strides in toilet tissue technology since my last visit. And though it took some convincing, I was happy to discover that the water was drinkable.

Paris had become a whole other city. Even the Parisians were nicer.

Okay, some of the change had happened within me. For a young kid from a small town, the pace and scale of Paris were a shock, especially after we'd been traveling through sweet Swiss villages. But after living in New York for eighteen years, I was used to the bustle of big-city living. And my eyes had become accustomed to city dirt. *Spotless* was a relative term. Sure, Paris was cleaner than it had been, but it was still only marginally cleaner than New York. I also came to realize that maybe Parisians weren't rude and impatient; maybe *all* city people were rude and impatient. What could be more annoying than trying to navigate around a cluster of thirteen gawking American teenagers when you're late for work? I'd have sighed and rolled my eyes, too. Hell, maybe I'd even have flung a rat.

I understood Parisians now, and I liked their city. A lot.

When my friend asked if I wanted to go to Paris again six months later, the answer was a ready yes. Three years into it, I'd racked up twice as many visits and was getting the hang of the city. Paris was easy; you could get there in seven hours. Italy was an odyssey by comparison. And unlike Rome, a delirious ramble of streets and alleys, Paris was totally manageable. By my second visit I had mastered the Métro.

Ten years after that first trip with my friend, I'd formed a bond with the city. Every quartier was now part of my vernacular—and Paris was now part of my psyche. All my vacations were monomaniacally Parisian; I was living a whole other life there. It was always the same: the minute I landed in Paris, like the flick of a switch, my Paris self would turn on. I dressed differently, spoke differently, was more creative, more daring, more spontaneous. I had my Paris friends, ate my Paris food, moved at my Paris pace. I even smoked once in a while, something I never did in New York.

It wasn't affectation; it was genuine mutation.

Maybe it had something to do with the pull of the Rose Line—the old prime meridian that ran under the city. I don't know, but Paris realigned me. I needed it the way some people need a visit to the spa. I always returned to New York a better person than I was when I left.

Paris had crept up on me, crept into me. Now I couldn't imagine my life without it.

It was love at long last.

Three

Who Was This Person?

By the first anniversary of Ma's death, I was six months into my "Paris apartment porn" addiction. Up to now, I'd kept it to myself, but that was about to change.

I'd booked a trip to Paris to mark the year since Ma passed; there was only one place I wanted to be on such a day: 3,600 miles away from the things I was already avoiding, such as paying my dead mother's medical bills and facing family and friends who kept asking when we were going to add her name to the family headstone. There was also our childhood home to deal with, which sat untouched since the day Ma died.

I wasn't ready to deal with any of it, so instead, I spent the day with some friends in Montmartre and lit a candle for my mother in Sacré-Coeur.

The next day, while walking along Paris's Coulée Verte, an elevated park once part of the now-defunct Bastille train line, I confessed my guilty pleasure of online apartment hunting to my friend Fabien. I fully expected him to laugh. After all, it was pretty ridiculous. Instead, he took my hand and walked me into the nearest real estate agency, Agence Immobilière Bastille.

That's how it began.

I have an uncle who's a Science of Mind minister who always

told me that if you put your dream out there, the universe will respond. The instant you tell people about your dream, you become accountable—and that's a powerful motivator.

"I'd prefer two rooms, but a studio is okay if the layout is good and there's storage . . ."

Was that me talking?

"Older building, because the resale value is better. High ceilings . . . ornate molding, parquet floors, and a fireplace. Most important: good light, an elevator, and a well-maintained building in a safe area."

Yep, definitely my mouth moving. But only the hopeful side of my brain was engaged. The rest of me was watching horrified.

"Budget?" the agent asked.

It was just a teensy two-syllable word, but it spun me around like he'd whacked me in the head with it. Reality checks are like that. Well? Did my dream have a price?

I threw out a number. Hearing it declared so definitively unnerved me.

"Or so," I added.

I didn't mean "give or take a few." "Or so" was just vague enough to give me a different kind of leeway: a way out. It kept one foot firmly planted in reality, because "or so" really meant "zero euros." Who was I kidding? Buying an apartment in Paris was for other people. Richer people. Braver people.

I left my contact information with the agent, and Fabien and I went to lunch. I could handle lunch. Lunch was something I could get my brain around.

Except there was an undeniable buzzing in my gut now.

The apartment was in a building on rue des Immeubles-Industriels, or "Street of Industrial Buildings." It was in a small district of identical structures dating from 1870 that originally housed manufacturing companies and workshops. Even today, about half are occupied by businesses. Imposing and masculine, with cast-iron colonnaded façades and rows of large arched windows, these buildings are a rare sight in Paris, where serpentine Haussmann freestone predominates.

The real estate agent had called offering a property in building number five. My friend Fabien was working, so he sent his boyfriend, Christian, for support, since he had experience in the Paris real estate game. Now two other people were involved.

Accountability is a bitch.

As I stood looking at the buildings lining the street, I remarked to Christian how much they reminded me of buildings in New York's SoHo district, an area famous for its own cast-iron factory buildings, which by the 1970s were mostly abandoned when manufacturing moved overseas. By this time, they had been reserved for artists, and the district was just beginning to make a name for itself. When I was a young girl, my parents brought my sister and me to tour these studios, whose use was designated only by small blue plaques labeled A.I.R. ("Artist in Residence"), posted to alert the Fire Department that someone was indeed living there. I imagined myself in one of these loft spaces, looking out through huge double-hung windows to the cobblestone street below.

"Wouldn't it be exciting to live like this?" Ma asked as we walked along Greene Street. The glint in her eye told me she wanted one of these places even more for herself. I wasn't surprised. When she was a teenager living in Buffalo, New York, in the 1950s, her dream was to be in Greenwich Village, painting in her own artist's studio, philosophizing with writers and hepcat jazz musicians, snapping her fingers in applause at a poetry reading in some coffeehouse on Waverly Place with the other Beatniks.

Except in 1950s Buffalo, young girls studied stenography and worked in offices where they would meet their husbands, then go on to settle down and have babies. So she did that.

That trip to SoHo with us was her way of imprinting her dream into my young head while it was still soft enough to accept the impression. Over the years, like a stage mom, she would continue to push me in the direction of her dreams. She wanted to be sure I would not repeat her mistake. This approach of hers was meant to inspire me, but it only made me inherit her desperate longing and fear of loss.

The opportunity for my SoHo loft would pass me by, as the excesses of the 1980s escalated the gentrification of downtown Manhattan at a dizzying pace. By the time I was living in New York as a young art student, I couldn't touch a square foot of SoHo real estate. The galleries had moved in, and then shortly thereafter, the chain stores. It was over before it began. Even many artists were pushed out of the very area they had made desirable.

Some thirty-odd years later, here I was on rue des Immeubles-Industriels. A district in another city in another country, but it pulsed with the same energy of a place on the brink of change. The buildings were still raw; a person would have to be prepared to rough it somewhat, but if you were willing to be a pioneer, you could make a really ripping investment.

On the ground floor of the building where I was about to see a large studio apartment, a brand-new gallery—the first of many to follow, no doubt—still smelled of fresh paint on its pristine white walls. The change had begun.

The agent arrived five minutes late—a lithe man in his late twenties, with big brown eyes and a pouty mouth that spoke an apology. I was forgiving; Christian was not, and told him so.

We entered the building, rode the elevator to the apartment. Except for spanking new windows, there was very little that didn't need to be updated: the cheap linoleum flooring; a bathroom and kitchen in ruins; questionable electric and plumbing. None of that mattered. I could see only the three floor-to-ceiling arched windows and the ten-foot ceiling crossed by painted cast-iron beams.

I saw only what it could be: cocktail parties with friends lounging on midcentury modern furniture; walls turned into an ad hoc gallery for my friends' artwork; the nine-foot Christmas tree I'd be able to fit inside.

I felt a rush. Could I do this?

Christian scrutinized my dream loft through narrowed eyes. He shook his head a few times. He knelt down and picked at the electric cables stapled to the baseboards, flipped switches, frowned at the toilet. He questioned the agent, the sharp consonants of his Parisian-accented French cutting the young man's sales swagger down to size.

"The floor is shit. The electric is shit," he said to the man. "The bathroom and kitchen must be completely redone. This needs at least fifty thousand euros' work."

My dream was a dump. It was all over.

Then Christian took me aside and, in English, said, "I think you should make an offer."

It took a second to register. Hadn't he just trashed the place? My heart thunked in my throat. This was it. Christian felt it, too; he knew it too: this was the right place at the right time—and with the right price tag, well below the average for the city. I would be getting in on the ground floor. If I had been dreaming up to now, the apartment hunt had just become a little more real—and possible. It didn't matter if I could afford it; I'd find a way. After all, this was what my mother had wanted for me. She was clearly orchestrating this from the great beyond, or wherever she was now.

The agent said something to Christian I didn't understand. Christian snapped a reply, threw his hands up. "C'est déjà fait," he said to me, banging his hands together.

I flinched. "What's already done?"

"The owner already accepted an offer. It's done," he said again. "It's sold. Let's go." He tugged on my arm and started for the door.

I pulled away. Sold?

I made him say it again. It couldn't be. This was what Ma had wanted.

I looked to the agent, to his pretty gaping mouth. His large brown eyes pleaded with us, but he had nothing to offer.

"It's sold?" I asked him.

He nodded somberly.

I wanted to slug that pretty mouth. That lying mouth. I asked him why he'd wasted my time.

"Because he had nothing to show you," Christian barked. "He still had the keys, and he thinks you're a prospect, so he showed you this to hook you. It's sold. It's done. Let's go."

This would not be my Paris apartment.

I should have been relieved. After all, I wasn't completely sure I was really doing this. Right?

But I wasn't relieved. Something in me had shifted. I'd put a foot in a new world where I could seize what I wanted, and I'd liked how it felt.

It was weeks after I had lost the apartment on rue des Immeubles-Industriels, and the days of fantasizing were long gone. By now my apartment hunt was no longer just about me alone in front of the glow of my computer in the wee hours. The more people I told, the more I heard "Good for you! How exciting! You deserve it!"— especially from those who'd witnessed what I'd been through.

I did deserve it, didn't I? A little happiness of my own?

I hadn't thought about how I was going to pay for an apartment in Paris. I hadn't thought any of it through. Sane people research their options before they invest in property, particularly overseas. But for me, it wasn't about an investment; it wasn't even really about Paris. This was pure self-preservation. I latched onto the idea of the apartment and let it drag me along.

My colleagues were my biggest cheerleaders. They'd gather around my computer screen to tour my latest finds, ooh-ing and ah-ing. My creative team would offer décor ideas or space-saving solutions for some of the tinier apartments I was considering, such as the two-hundred-square-foot studio on rue de la Roquette.

It seemed to inspire other people that I was reaching for something bigger for myself. The more I shared my crazy scheme, the more people began to invest in it, to contribute to it.

I became a community project.

Christian, back in Paris, had taken it upon himself to help me look for apartments—and he was serious, which meant I had to be serious. He would ask me to send him links to places I liked, and if he thought they looked promising, he would visit them and report back. He seemed to be enjoying himself:

> Building—7 out of 10; Apartment—10 out of 10; Neighborhood—3 out of 10. I must advise against this one. It is not safe for a young girl.

This was his report for a beauty on rue Crespin du Gast, fully renovated by an architect. It was all white: white walls, white floors. Also well below Paris market value, but that was because of the neighborhood, according to Christian. I passed on the place, but wondered if I'd missed out on an incredible opportunity in an up-and-coming area. Maybe if I'd seen the neighborhood for myself I'd have felt differently.

There was a spacious top-floor place on rue de Charonne, with a balcony, herringbone parquet floors, and marble fireplaces—the ultimate Parisian apartment, again at bargain prices. Christian saw signs of water damage from a possible building issue and raised a red flag—"Building: 4 out of 10." I passed on that one, too, but with regrets. What if that was supposed to be my Paris apartment?

I was getting itchy to pull the trigger.

The clincher was a large two-bedroom in the 18th arrondissement, in the north of the city, in a glorious Art Nouveau building that Christian went to see one Saturday. I'd set my alarm so I could ring him at five in the morning New York time to see what he'd thought of it. He was still in the apartment when I called, so I'd have to wait for his report. Was it a real ten-out-of-ten kind of place?

I was very optimistic about this one. It was laid out in a classic *étoile*, or star pattern—each room located off a large foyer. So elegant and so Parisian. The walls were edged with ornate molding; the eat-in kitchen was enormous. There was a walk-in closet, two bedrooms—it was perfection, and another bargain, though with a higher price tag than I'd wanted to pay. Still, it would be well worth it.

Thirty-five minutes after I called, Christian finally called back. "Okay, so I have seen it."

"And?"

"It's really quite nice. And the quartier is very good. Very safe. But—"

"But?"

"Well . . . it's dark."

Dark? How dark? Maybe it wasn't a big deal. My apartment in New York was dark, too. How bad could it be?

"I really can't recommend it."

It was *that* dark?

"It faces a very narrow courtyard. Your neighbors are just three meters away. It's very hard for sunlight to come in."

Well, that explains the bargain. Still, it was so incredible in every other way. Maybe if I could just see it in person. "Do you think I should come next weekend and visit it?"

Does he think I should what?

Who was this person I'd become?

"Well, if you think you want to," Christian said. "I agree. It's very hard to buy an apartment doing it like this. You just have to come here. We can get an agent and arrange many visits."

Yes, of course he was right. I absolutely had to do that because that's what you do when you're serious about buying property in Paris.

Well, I guess I was serious. Now.

Two weekends later I was on a plane. The plan: one day, six apartments.

I was in deep.

"Shopping spree in Paris this weekend. Bought some pâté, a shirt— oh, and this apartment."

This was my Facebook post when I arrived home from Paris. It included photos of a sweet sun-filled apartment with high ceilings, beautiful crown molding, and two enormous windows that opened onto an elegant, narrow street in the 11th arrondissement.

The apartment was the last of the six we'd seen. It was St. Patrick's Day and I'd arrived in Paris at eight thirty in the morning. I'd told myself I wasn't leaving Paris without an apartment. Well, half of me felt this way; the other half was asking, *What the hell are you doing?*

There were so many people involved now that my commitment had become partly about saving face. I guess this is what my uncle had meant about accountability. And since I would be turning around and leaving Paris the next morning, I had to make this day count—but I was up against it. The problem was my budget. Even though, to me, it was an enormous sum, the pickings for the price I could afford were slim: an apartment over a Renault garage that needed a hundred thousand dollars' worth of work; a bland ground-floor studio in a soulless 1980s building.

The two closest contenders still had issues, but if I was serious about leaving Paris with an apartment, did it matter? I had a puny budget in an expensive city; there would always be a trade-off. Maybe it just came down to which trade-off I could live with.

What was I waiting for, a sign?

The apartment was the size of a hotel room and didn't check nearly any of the boxes on my wish list, but it was move-in ready and one hundred fifty thousand dollars cheaper than any of the other apartments we'd seen. Technically, if I was willing to part with some of my retirement and inheritance money, I could even pay cash for it. This thing was actually possible.

According to the agent, the seller was American, too, and also in magazine publishing. She was living a life parallel to mine—visiting Paris often, maintaining a life here. A hell of a coincidence.

I took another look around the place. Even at five in the evening on a rainy day in March, light flooded the space. It had been renovated within the last few years, had plenty of storage, a washing machine, new heating and windows, and a workable, modern kitchen unit in shiny cobalt blue.

My mother always had a blue kitchen. Blue for Saint Mary. This was a must for any good Catholic: one room in blue. It made sense that Ma chose the kitchen because, to an Italian, the kitchen is the heart of the home.

The French call it a *coup de coeur*, the thing that grabs your heart and says, *yes!*

I made an offer on the spot. I'd worry about the rest later.

My offer was accepted three days before my sister and I were about to empty our childhood home and ready it for sale. My new Paris home couldn't have come at a better time.

Four

Destroy a Home, Build a Home

I think you should be aware of how often you talk about the past," a friend told me over lunch one day. He was concerned for my state of mind. It seemed I held too dearly the objects and mementos of my life and family.

Sure, I talked about my mother a lot, but she'd only been dead a little over a year. What was so great about the future anyway? All I saw ahead were epic weather events courtesy of global warming, corporate domination, and tasteless engineered food.

Nostalgia is in my blood. My mother was a passionate teacher of history and a lover of all things "was." I, too, prefer the bygone, and I'm prone to waxing wistful over the end of something even as I'm living it—cherishing, hanging on.

But to my friend, this was a gross defect. "I'm worried about you," he said. "It's not healthy to be always thinking about the past."

Apparently I was out of touch; my mind was decaying, smothering under layers of moth-eaten dreams, mildewed memories blocking the way for the New to enter and be embraced.

I've been surrounded by the Old my whole life, and have loved it. My grandmother's 1840s Italianate home in downtown Buffalo was a treasure trove of nostalgia: the cabinet of family photos in the front hall parlor, the wooden radio as big as a chest of drawers, the eighteenth-century mahogany secretary in the sitting room that you had to open "just so" or it would unhinge and break a toe. And my favorite of all old good things: the black-and-white 1920s enamel-top kitchen table where my grandmother made her gnocchi. Still fresh in my memory is the cool metal surface I would lean upon, enrapt, watching her ricing the potatoes into the dough, then kneading the mixture together and rolling it out. She'd form the dumplings with a flick of her finger, using a machine-like speed and precision that only years of practiced repetition could produce. This was all seared into my mind, and I wanted to linger there at will when I needed to. So sue me.

Our mother's older sister, our aunt Nicky, died just two weeks after Ma, taking many old family recipes with her. There was no one left to ask about our lineage, or to help me remember my first Christmas.

My sister and I, along with our cousins, were the older generation now. We had to be the keepers of memory for the younger ones. But I was reluctant, still feeling like the baby of the family, still hanging on.

You should be aware of how often you talk about the past . . .

The past was safe and familiar. I liked it there. That was where Ma was still walking and talking, and cooking roasted chicken. Filling the house with her huge guffaw of a laugh. In the evergreen past of my mind, the teacups still clinked in the china cabinet as I ran through Gramma's dining room, headed toward the kitchen, where everyone was crowded around the table drinking coffee and talking much too loudly over one another's conversations. My aunt Mary was still able to take me to tea at the Albright-Knox Art Gallery. My dad and I were still sitting in church, my head on his shoulder after we'd recovered from a bad case of the giggles.

These memories were all I had left. How could anyone ask me to give them up? Should I have just blazed ahead and, like Robert Moses or Haussmann, cut a ruthless swath through the historic row houses in my mind?

Maybe people mean to ease your pain when they tell you not to look back, but to someone missing a tangible connection to a loved one they've lost, it feels like deprivation. Cruel.

Still, whether I wanted to or not, I would be forced to let go of the past. My sister and I were about to empty our childhood home so we could put it on the market.

We'd procrastinated for over a year, which we quickly realized was a huge mistake. We should have done it immediately after Ma died, when we were still numb. We'd set ourselves up for a punishing process.

My sister, Maria, moved into the house. I took as much time off as I could, stretching out my vacation days into three- and four-day weekends. We ordered boxes and packing supplies, a Dumpster. I cleaned out a junk drawer in the kitchen. The front hall closet. Maria bought groceries. We drank wine. The first week passed.

The next week, an auction company came by and appraised our family treasures. Apparently, they weren't worth as much to them as they were to us. We tried to empty Ma's closet, but her perfume still clung to her sweaters. Instead, I started on the garage. Maria made our meals, talked on the phone. Drank Jack and Coke.

It seemed easier for us to go through our own stuff, so on week three we tackled our bedrooms. They'd been kept perfectly intact since the days we lived at home: my collection of birthday angel figurines remained on my dresser, every school memento tucked away in the drawers. Our rooms were shrines to our childhood, the porcelain nameplates still on the doors: MARIA'S ROOM, LISA'S ROOM. Rummaging through our pasts reintroduced us to our younger selves. Maria appeared in the doorway of my room wearing neon New Wave wraparound sunglasses. I trumped her with my KISS Army iron-on patch. She called me a geek, probably the exact word she used the day the patch came in the mail. We laughed our way through that weekend. By Sunday, I'd finished my room, but Maria had gotten only halfway through hers. I noticed she kept stopping to talk on the phone, or hide out on the front porch.

Week four, we sold Ma's car to her best friend. I went through the dining and living rooms, but I had to force Maria to make choices about what she wanted to take. It was hard to get her to focus. She'd pack a few things and then wander off. Always on the phone, or cooking, shopping for food. By myself, I packed up six boxes of dishes, glasses, and tablecloths for storage.

Still, there was so much to do, and it wasn't getting done. I made schedules of what we needed to accomplish: basement next week, attic the week after. I'd beg Maria to just do one dresser or one cabinet while I was working in New York. She'd promise to do it, but when I'd arrive at the house, I'd find nothing had been done. It wasn't laziness; she was paralyzed by pain. I'd have to be the bad guy, the whip cracker, making up for lost time. She resisted at every turn, especially anytime I wanted to do something that would radically alter the house, such as stack the growing number of boxes in the living room or start emptying the kitchen. "I have to live here!" she'd say.

Who was living here? We were moving out, weren't we?

While I was clearing out the attic and the basement, she was happily nesting, preparing our meals in the kitchen, saying how good it was to be back home, that she was just starting to appreciate the beauty of the area.

Maria was digging in as I was digging out. And we were both going out of our minds. I finally understood what my friend meant when he said that hanging on to the past was unhealthy.

I thought our mother's death would be the hardest thing to bear, but this was much, much worse. It was as if Ma and Dad were dying all over again. We had to go through forty years of accumulated memory. With each object we discovered, we would be forced to relive the specific memory attached to it, then agonize over whether we should keep the item, sell it, or throw it away: a pair of childhood lefty scissors; our father's diary from World War II we never knew existed; our mother's sorority bracelet with the names of her oft-talked-about "sisters" engraved on each segment; our childhood toys, *every* last one; greeting cards going back fifty years. I found corsages that Dad had given Ma when they were courting; all my sister's childhood drawings, notated by my mother with things like MARIA'S FIRST PAINTING, AGE 4. They saved everything. Scores of treasures, of memories, pieces of our lives, snatches of who we were, who we are. Our story in stuff.

We repeated this emotional ritual hundreds of times over nearly a hundred days.

And while I was tossing pieces of one home into a twenty-yard-long Dumpster, I was reviewing blueprints for another. The contract on my Paris apartment had been signed, and I'd hired an architect and contractor to plan a renovation that would transform the space from two small rooms to one large studio. Everyone said I shouldn't take on such a project from more than 3,600 miles away, but I was on a mission. I couldn't control the profound sense of loss overtaking me, but I could control what color tiles I wanted in the bathroom, or where to put the electrical outlets.

I poured all my energy into the renovation, all my angst, too, sending nearly a hundred emails to my contractor, another hundred to my architect: diagrams, ideas, lists, reminders. Questions, so many questions. Was the electric panel sufficient if I wanted to put in an oven eventually? What was the maximum depth I could have for the bathroom sink? Should I consider all new flooring, and what was the difference in price? I obsessed over every minute detail of the renovation, gripping the project by the reins and steering it as mightily as I could.

It was the one source of hope I had, the one part of my life that was forward-looking.

Planning the decoration of the apartment brought some small joy to both Maria and me. After a long day of dust and tears, we'd sit with our glasses of wine in front of my computer and do some virtual window shopping—dreaming, planning. We looked forward to it each day. My Paris apartment was a 258-square-foot life raft in the midst of it all. Maybe this is what had driven me to buy it in the first place. Something inside me knew I'd need to be building a new home in order to survive dismantling an old one.

The day we packed up the kitchen was by far the hardest. There was a reason the kitchen was physically in the center of the house: it had been the center of Ma's life, and ours. I understood now why Maria had spent so much time in there, cooking while I was taking the rest of the rooms apart. As long as she was making meals, the house was ours. No other room embodied Ma more. Emptying those cupboards was emptying Ma's spirit.

Most of it ended up in our boxes.

By early June, we'd finished wrapping up what we wanted to take, and arranged for the auction house and Salvation Army to pick up what was left. The last thing I did before I left the house was pull our nameplates off the bedroom doors. *We don't live here anymore.* It was time for other children to create their own memories in those rooms.

We filled a ten-by-twelve-foot storage unit with nearly seventy boxes, but one box was destined for another location. Labeled FOR PARIS, it held a few precious memories—a bit of the past to decorate my future: the red-and-white tablecloth we ate our Valentine's Day dinners on; a small gold-framed Degas print from my childhood bedroom; a tray that sat on the kitchen counter all our lives, which I had just realized had a Paris street scene painted on it. Now it would sit on the counter in another blue kitchen, where new memories would be made.

While on a bus in Nashville, Tennessee, an email popped up on my phone. The subject: "You are now the proud owner of a Parisian apartment!"

It was 6:33 P.M. on June 5. I was wearing white pants and a sheer pink tunic top. You don't forget the details of a moment like that.

A proxy in Paris had signed the documents of sale for me while I was attending a conference for my company. It's a peculiar thing not to be present while hundreds of thousands of dollars are being handed over. Maybe that's why I was able to do it. In fact, the entire sale had been handled by the agent, who just told me what to do and when. Back in New York, I had mostly gone about my life and trusted everything would go according to plan in Paris. I was forced to let go, and the more I did, the more things got done.

This apartment was proving to be more than a place to live; it was teaching me how to live.

My mind had been occupied with the conference all day, and I'd forgotten it was the day of the closing. Then, en route to a dinner event, while checking emails during a few minutes of downtime, there it was.

"I am now the proud owner of a Parisian apartment!" I shot up from my seat, phone aloft, the universal sign for "I've got mail."

Applause and whoops of joy filled the bus—a big, fat "Attagirl!" underscoring the accomplishment. My colleagues had been with me through my heartbreak; it only seemed right that they should share in the joy of the moment. That made it all the sweeter.

I had an impulse to call Ma.

Three days earlier I'd locked the front door of her home and said good-bye. Today it was all about what lay ahead.

A few weeks later I headed to Paris to oversee the renovation, and shop for décor for my *petit nid parisien*, my "little Parisian nest." I'd spent the last few weeks online researching furnishings with the decisiveness of an interior designer. While my apartment in New York is more of an ad hoc affair, full of years of accumulated antiques and castoffs from various relatives, the Paris apartment could start from square one. I had a very clear vision: a mix of clean modern lines with a few nods to old Paris. I made a modest budget, created a look book, pulled paint and fabric swatches, and compiled a list of stores to visit. Done and done. I'd never been so fearless, so decisive—even in metrics, even in French. Normally, I agonized over every decision, researching something for months, often never even pulling the trigger. Maybe I was afraid of regretting a wrong choice—but not anymore.

Now all I seemed to do was pull triggers and worry about the outcome later, or not at all. Yes, yes, yes. It was all about yes.

But when I saw the apartment for the first time as a new homeowner, it was more like "oh no."

"Holy crap, this is so freaking small," I said, choking on plaster dust and stepping over construction debris. My contractor, Aiden, a lanky South African with a boyish face, cocked his head, confused.

My heart started to pound in my chest. I wasn't sure what had happened, but somehow my dream home had shrunk about a hundred square feet.

The last time I'd seen the place in the flesh was back in March, and that had been for only thirty minutes. After that, I'd had to subsist on the agency's photos, which, as it turned out, were very craftily shot. During those months, those photos had helped me forget the words I'd uttered when I first saw the place: "Shit, this is tiny!"

Now I was saying it again, and it was pretty much all I could say. Shit! Shit! Shit!

What the hell had I bought?

"Didn't you see this in person before you bought it?" Aiden asked me, still confounded by my shock and horror.

"Yeah, but . . . wow . . . I dunno . . . I guess it looks different empty. Or something."

"You're not happy with the work? Something wrong?" Aiden's face screwed up, his brows knit. It seemed that worry was his default emotion. In our phone conversations during the planning, worry always tugged on his voice. I found that reassuring. Worry equaled care, conscientiousness. He worried about my budget more than I did, about the tiniest change that might cost twenty euros more. And my feeling was that since I had enough to worry about, when it came to the renovation, I'd let him worry for the both of us.

There was nothing wrong with the work; it was impeccable—what was done, that is. The rest was in shambles: tiles ripped out of the bathroom; a huge trench in the floor where a wall used to be; the wood-paneled door, now useless, flung on a heap of debris. I felt a pang of guilt about that door. I've always loved old French doors, their lever doorknobs mounted elbow high. Even before I had an apartment in Paris, I used to shop for doorknobs for my imaginary doors at Bazar de l'Hôtel de Ville, BHV—my favorite of *les grands magazins*, Paris's department stores. I'd fondle dozens of models, but always favored the classic brass or porcelain lever style. I promised myself I would have a door handle just like that in my Paris apartment one day.

Then again, no. You'd need a door for that, and I'd just ripped out mine.

The apartment didn't need to be renovated, not really, but it wasn't exactly perfect, either. The living space was too small, and the bedroom was too big. The previous owner compensated by putting a sofa next to the bed, like in a dorm. Sure, it was fine for the scores of students she'd rented to, but it wasn't fine for me. So, like Reagan in Berlin, I decreed, "Tear down this wall!" We'd open the space and create a small sleeping nook.

That should have been enough for me, but it wasn't. I decided I couldn't get past the red tile racing stripe in the bathroom, running down the back of the shower and along the floor toward the door. It screamed at me, that angry red stripe, so it, too, had to go.

And as long as we were tearing out stuff, that finger bowl of the bathroom sink? Gone. The lighting, too, didn't hold up to scrutiny. Dated disc-like sconces hung on every wall of the apartment, yet gave no light. Sconces made me think of a funeral home, so the sconces had to go. An antique crystal chandelier hanging over the living room was more what I had in mind, so the rewiring began.

I knew I could just as easily have thrown a coat of paint on the walls and made do. Making do was something I was good at. In fact, I come from a long line of make-do people—do the best with what you have and be grateful you have it. I could have bought red-trimmed towels for the bathroom to match the stripe, found more attractive sconces, put a screen between the bed and the sofa. I could have done all those things, and it would have been perfectly livable.

But that was before Ma died. The new me, the me I was becoming, didn't want to make do with someone else's crap. I wanted to customize the apartment to suit my needs, my wishes. Ma made do all her life, never realizing she was worth more.

I'd already taken a huge leap of faith to buy an apartment in another country. What was one small hop to make it perfect?

Didn't I deserve that?

But now, seeing the apartment with its jagged, gaping wounds made me queasy. The fixer, the one with the broom who sweeps up chaos, was sweating in the middle of the chaos she'd made of her perfect little jewel. I was suddenly filled with shame: it was as if I'd taken an antique vase and willfully flung it to the floor, sending it shattering irreparably into a million shards. I couldn't see what the apartment would become; I could see only what it used to be, what it would never be again. I'd killed it.

With my luck, something would happen, some cataclysmic event that would prevent the workers from finishing the job, and I'd be stuck with this heap of rubble forever. It would serve me right for demolishing a perfectly good home. Who did I think I was, taking on a renovation, a make-do girl like me? If I'd done a simple, inexpensive paint job, I'd have been moving in right now.

". . . paint, Lisa?"

I turned away from my poor dead door to Aiden fanning through a book of paint chips.

"You wanna choose a color for the accent wall?" he asked. "And did you decide which wall gets it?"

I blinked, snapping to. Which wall should get the accent color?

Looking around the apartment, at the two huge windows, which were in full view now that the wall was gone, I knew I'd made the right decision to renovate. I walked over to my new closet, already framed out and covered in wallboard, and ran my hand over the surface, which was still chalky and raw.

Aiden tapped at a mark on the wallboard. "We're gonna put the dimmer switch here. Cool?"

That dimmer switch was going to light up my chandelier. "Perfect," I said, eyeing the wiring hanging from the ceiling, waiting.

Actually, now that I was looking at everything, I saw that they'd done quite a bit of work to the apartment: run all the electric, restored the molding, smoothed the walls so they looked almost new. My home was starting to take shape in my mind: hope amid the ruins.

Like my life.

I would never have bought the apartment in Paris when my mother was alive; I wouldn't have had the courage even to tell her about the idea. I learned my lesson about that.

On a Mother's Day weekend several years before, I was visiting Ma. It had started out wonderfully. We planted her garden and did a little antique shopping—all our favorite things. Then, suddenly, it went sour over Mother's Day brunch.

I started talking about my voice lessons, something that had become an important part of my life. Singing, even more than writing, has always been a passion of mine. Several years before, I had started studying voice for fun, but I was now training in earnest as a classical singer. My coach believed I had the talent for a career in opera, and I was beginning to believe it, too. At my lesson the Friday before Mother's Day, my coach introduced me to an agent who was interested in signing me. It was a thrilling development, and I wanted to surprise my mother with the news.

Ma turned on me as if I'd attacked her. Her pretty face constricted; her large, brown eyes narrowed. "What do you want to do, sing at the *Met*?"

It was all in the tone, a dart laced with venom, targeted right at my insecure heart. It wasn't a question; it was a challenge: Who do you think you are?

I thought, *You won't do this to me again. You won't cut me down now. Not this time.* I took a deep breath and affirmed, "Yes. That's exactly what I'm going to do."

Even as the words were in my mouth, I knew I didn't believe them. I'd never sing at the Metropolitan Opera, because my mother had pushed that button in me, the Off button. This wasn't the first time; it wasn't the thousandth time. It was the hundred-thousandth time.

The sad thing was my mother was my biggest fan. She brought all her friends to see my performances—Musetta in *La Bohème*, Rosina in *The Barber of Seville*, my concert at Carnegie Hall's Weill Recital Hall—front row, tears in her eyes, so proud. Yet when it came to my breaking out, to really shooting for the big time, she'd pulled the emotional rug out from under me. If I became successful, would I leave her all alone in New Jersey? If I surpassed her, would that be worse? Would it make her invisible, insignificant? Would it be the ultimate betrayal on my part?

Ma had always inspired us to think bigger, but when we had an idea of a life outside her comfort zone, she would somehow put the kibosh on it, stir up doubt. Her limitations became ours. I know she didn't want that for us, but it happened all the same.

I had put my life on hold for my mother; her death set it back in motion.

In August, after the renovation and decoration of the apartment was complete, I went to stay in my new home for the first time.

When I opened the door, I wasn't prepared for what I found on the other side, although I should have been. Hadn't I planned every inch, chosen every stitch of furniture, approved the location of every electrical outlet?

I'd never realized a dream before, not a doozy like this one. Sure, I'd dreamed big, but it was always "out there" somewhere. One day. Longing was a part of who I was. I stowed the big dreams in my head so I had something to reflect on when life became unbearable. Dreaming was a survival mechanism, not an action plan. My life had been all about "one day."

All of a sudden I was in the middle of "one day."

Stupefied, I took it all in. My carry-on bag plunked on the floor, having slipped from a hand that went slack and shaky as I broke down.

The apartment was exactly as I had envisioned it: every chair, every piece of fabric. For months it had been just an architectural drawing, a collage of concepts, a string of emails. Now I was standing in the middle of it, the smell of fresh paint making it real, sunlight kissing it from the two floor-to-ceiling windows, now draped in gray striped silk curtains. This was not just an apartment; this was evidence of the greatness I could achieve.

For the first time in my life I had taken responsibility for my own happiness.

Paris was the perfect place to lay the groundwork for the next phase of my life. It was the one spot on the map that was all mine, totally unto me with no connection, obligation, or judgment from any of the usual sources. A place where I could be myself, where anything was possible.

And buying an apartment in Paris was investing in me, planting my standard in the world.

This was my time, my turn.

PART 2

....

Learning to Live Like a Local

(ONE VACATION AT A TIME)

Five

Here I Am in No-Man's-Land

I hadn't looked that closely at my neighborhood before I bought the apartment. I wasn't even sure where the neighborhood was at the time I made the offer because it was at the end of a long day and we'd wandered all over the 11th arrondissement. I figured it was somewhere in the vicinity of the trendy Bastille district.

It wasn't. My brand-new Paris apartment was in an area I'd earlier referred to as "No-Man's-Land," a far eastern part of Paris where I'd been exactly once, many years before, to meet a friend for dinner on rue du Faubourg Saint-Antoine.

At the time, I was staying in a hotel near Saint-Germain-des-Prés, a lovely if not posh part of town. To get to the restaurant, I had to cross the river and trek clear across town to Place de la Nation, a massive traffic circle with ten avenues branching off like spokes from the hub of a wheel. When I exited the Métro station, the expanse of the circle paralyzed me. Which way was I supposed to go? Traffic zoomed all around; people brushed past. A small gang of young men huddled by the Métro—who, to this New Yorker, looked as if they were dealing drugs—turned their attention to me. It was time to move, so I took off in a random direction.

Fifteen minutes later, I was still walking. I'd passed eight avenues, then nine, ten, growing more anxious as it grew dark—lost in a city I thought I knew.

This was not the Paris I'd come to love. This Paris had blocks of modern apartment complexes, double-wide avenues, and big-box stores. Instead of the ubiquitous Haussmann structures, with their elegant wrought-iron balconies, here the buildings were plain-faced, tired, and scrawled in graffiti. Maybe I wasn't in Paris anymore. Maybe I'd gone too far on the train and ended up in the Bronx.

Twenty minutes into my search for this elusive street called Faubourg Saint-Antoine, I'd now walked completely around the circle, back to where I'd started—like those nightmares where you run and run but never get anywhere. The gang of drug-selling hoods eyed me anew.

I might have retreated into the Métro, back to the safety of my familiar Left Bank neighborhood, until I saw, directly in front of me, a street sign announcing my folly: rue du Faubourg Saint-Antoine.

If I had just walked right out of the station instead of left, I would have been there in thirty seconds. I could feel the neighborhood taunting me. *Take zat, you seelly, stoopid vooman!*

I was pretty sure I'd never come to this corner of Paris again.

Then I went and bought a piece of it.

When most people buy property in Paris, they opt for districts in the center of town, where the real estate values are higher, with characteristics one thinks of as quintessentially Parisian: nineteenth-century white stone buildings with their sloping gray Mansard roofs and filigreed balconies; cafés with enamel-top tables facing ancient cobbled squares. Not me. Nope, I plunked my hard-earned money right smack on No-Man's-Land.

On the first day in my apartment, I explored the streets of my new neighborhood. All around me, bleak 1970s apartment buildings imposed themselves like alien spaceships that had crash-landed on the old streets. Uninspired and utilitarian, their brutish ugliness unnerved me; they were out of place in a city I loved for its delicate beauty.

Many of the basic ingredients of the classic Parisian neighborhood were missing here. Not a single decent café could be found nearby, just a lot of takeout places with gaudy Plexiglas shop signs screaming their odd fare: PIZZA-BAGEL-SHAWARMA-HAMBURGER. Where was I? The boardwalk at the Jersey Shore?

The brasserie on my corner had its best years behind it, and served wine from a box that had sat there who knows how long. Empty most of the day, except for a few old men drinking at the chipped Formica bar, it had all the charm of truck stop.

Forget about buying bread every morning at the corner *boulangerie*. There wasn't one within five blocks. But, hey, if I wanted to take up smoking, I'd have had no shortage of *tabacs*, tobacco bars. There were *three*, just a few streets apart, with flashy neon track lighting and an all-male clientele who stood around on the sidewalk smoking and drinking. The heat of their gazes burned into me as I passed.

Stranded in No-Man's-Land.

This was not at all what I had in mind when I bought an apartment in Paris. This was what happened when you made an emotional, split-second decision on real estate. The apartment would probably never turn a profit, and now I was pretty sure I'd overpaid for it. Foiled by my own impulsiveness.

Take zat, you seelly, stoopid vooman!

The neighborhood stood in sharp contrast to my sweet apartment, and my cozy street—just one block long, with an ivy-covered alley off to one side that led to a small green park. An unmistakable buttery aroma of something like baking sugar cookies hung in the air. An olfactory phantom maybe, a sign from my mother that I was home.

Sounds of music filled the air, too. In this case, I knew they came from the school across the street, a Parisian version of New

York's High School of Performing Arts, the school made famous in *Fame*, a film that was an inspiration for me as a kid dreaming of a career in theater. Was this another sign that Ma meant for me to be here? Was she ensuring that her daughter, a singer and musician, would be surrounded by music and applause?

Signs began to appear everywhere that maybe my mother had picked this corner of Paris for me. Was I trying to compensate for my disappointment in the neighborhood's lack of character? Possibly. But it wasn't lost on me, either, that my house number was the same as my mother's birth date and that the apartment had a blue kitchen, as hers had had. If Ma handpicked this place for me, drab surroundings and all, it was up to me to discover why.

Had I bought the apartment for a real estate investment? No. It was never about creating a vacation rental or a making a quick flip for profit. I was buying a piece of the city that had become a haven, taking a leap from despair to hope. When you're taking any kind of a leap, you want a safety net, and this district was close to friends. My dearest friend, Geoffrey—pronounced ZJHAW-fray—was just a few streets away, where he shared an apartment with his longtime boyfriend, Christophe. That fit the most important criterion of all.

Geoffrey and I had met six years earlier, when he was managing a tea shop on rue de Seine, near my hotel in the 6th arrondissement. It was the only store open on a desolate winter Sunday, and its bold, warm colors drew me in. Geoffrey offered me tea, and that was it. An hour later, we'd talked about nearly everything that mattered to both of us.

He was the opposite of every Parisian stereotype: unguarded, optimistic to the point of naïve, with an easy smile and a generous nature. A force majeure, he had unquenchable energy, an enormous laugh, and even larger gestures. I had the feeling that to be in Geoffrey's life was to be swept up in his current, both participant and spectator.

"I don't know eef you will think this ees strange," Geoffrey said that day, "but I feel very strong we 'ave a connection."

We did, a bond that was immediate and lasting. He calls me his *p'tite soeur*—his little sister—and signs his notes to me as "Your French Brother." That I was now just five minutes away from him made us squeal like eight-year-old girls.

During that first week in my new apartment, Geoffrey was having one of his epic birthday parties. A visual artist, he always created themed events, with a "photo call," a wall covered in a pattern of his trademark handlebar mustache where we'd pose for photos like celebrities at a Hollywood premiere. It wasn't meant to be taken too seriously; this was just Geoffrey's way of celebrating life in his usual big way.

The last time I went to his birthday party was just a few months after my mother died. Then, I traveled from a hotel across town. This time, I simply walked out my own door and in five minutes was at Geoffrey's home.

This was my Paris life now. I'd created this for myself.

My proximity to friends meant that someone was popping over often, and in that case it was best to keep some wine and snacks on hand at all times. My New York social life had stopped dead, especially since my dining table was piled high with paperwork from my mother's estate, but here in Paris, it was being resuscitated. Or maybe my entire life was.

People came over for breakfast, lunch, and dinner. My space-saving table for four turned out to be too small. It was never only one or two of us; we were at least five, sometimes seven or eight around the too-tiny table—someone sitting on my stepstool, another on the taboret. No one minded. Parisians are used to compact spaces. All the better to gather close. We'd crowd around the food, our chatter and Geoffrey's huge laugh bouncing off the buildings on my narrow street.

For me, these friends gave a heart and soul to No-Man's-Land.

They charted a treasure map of the area, revealed its secrets hidden under the patina, such as some of the best, and oldest, cafés in Paris, or the *boulangerie* well worth the extra ten-minute walk. If I was missing Ma's cooking, rue de Charonne was where I could find Italian specialty shops. The best place for quality meats: the kosher butcher right up the street.

If I ever tired of French food, however unlikely that seemed, there was a Chinese noodle shop near rue du Faubourg Saint-Antoine—yes, the same elusive street that was my nemesis years before—where you could watch the chef make noodles to order. He'd pull and whip the dough in the air until into transformed into long, thin strands, which broke apart and tumbled into a pot of boiling water.

The greatest treasure in the area: Marché d'Aligre, home to a large street market and food district. This wonderland of French culinary riches turned you into a wide-eyed Julia Child. Riotous with vegetables, cheeses, breads, meats, fish, fowl, and flowers, it overflowed with shoppers on market day, each heaping their straw baskets and caddies with their booty, the obligatory baguette peeking out over the top like something out of a postcard. Only, this was real Paris life.

That was the best thing about No-Man's-Land: it was locals only. That meant *zero* tourists, something perceptible straight away. The local businesses were all suited to everyday life, instead of the high-end fashion boutiques I was used to in the center of the city. There were places to get your shoes repaired, your keys copied, your laundry washed. Prices were dirt cheap, too. In fact, I suffered reverse sticker shock. In the window of a clothing shop on rue de la Roquette, a price tag on a skirt made me look twice: twenty-five euros. Didn't they mean *one hundred* twenty-five?

Nope. Not here, where real Parisians lived and shopped. Here, four-euro glasses of wine were the norm, and that stuff from the box turned out to be pretty damn decent.

For years I'd complained about the loss of the local feel of my

New York City neighborhood, now one of Manhattan's "It" districts. It's impossible to get a table in the nearby restaurants. Sleek apartment towers supplanted the old carriage houses as everything went upscale and commercialized. Much of Paris was also succumbing to this, but here in No-Man's-Land, a little village still existed, untouched by developers, and time.

The last patch of real Paris. It wasn't clear how long it would last, but it was unmistakable that No-Man's-Land was a gem. Here was somewhere a person could really live, get to know the neighbors, and lay down roots. I could have a quality of life in this neighborhood that I didn't even have in New York: something intimate and personal.

Was I ready for that?

· Six ·

I'm Sure If I Could Only
Understand You,
I'd Like You

Bonjour, fawfaw faw?" the proprietor of a clothing boutique greeted me. *"Ah, oui, faw, faw! Fawfaw, faw?"*

My gut tightened. Please, dear God, what was she saying? Was it about the weather? Were they having a special sale? Was there ink on my face?

Squeezing my lips together in what I hoped was a smile, but was more likely a grimace, I tipped my head to one side like a dog who hears his master's voice but grasps only sounds of intent. I'd caught about every third word—promises of meaning but, like the proverbial carrot, dangling before me just beyond my reach.

How is it that my French wasn't up to the task of local life in Paris? I'd done pretty well, up to now, ordering in restaurants, telling taxi drivers where to take me, buying shoes at Bazar de l'Hôtel de Ville—you know, the important stuff. But my neighborhood, where no one spoke a lick of English, was a whole new world.

This was getting-to-know-you French, talking-about-politics-in-a-bar French, making-a-deeper-connection French—and all I could make out was "Faw faw faw."

What's French for "I'm totally screwed"?

It's a terrible thing, being on the outside of a language. So much going on around you, a world of conversation, and there you are, barred from entering. Your ignorance is like the bouncer at a cool club who won't let you in.

Over the years, each time I came to Paris, despite six years of what I thought was excellent French training, I still heard "Fawfaw" from passersby on the street, "Fawfaw" at the café table next to me.

You'd be surprised at how much the chatter around you connects you to your world. These snippets of small talk are snatches of life that keep you part of a community. It's the difference between being invited to share in an event and being an observer.

I often vacationed by myself in Paris, and my inability—or hesitation—to make idle chitchat of any kind isolated me. To cope, I would have lengthy conversations with myself in my head, a continuous banter that drowned out the loneliness.

I think I'll turn left here. Not sure where it will go, but what the hell? I wonder if I should get money from that ATM, since it's right here. I do need more money. Oh, look, macaroons!

By the end of my vacation, I'd feel as if I were going nuts. Still, I'd always return to New York taking home only the best memories of Paris, the isolation forgotten like labor pains, thanks to a suitcase full of Paris goodies.

Now I had an apartment here. The isolation would not be able to be dismissed so easily; it would move in with me if I didn't *parler français* with the locals. It wasn't just about functioning here; I wanted to *belong* here. How much time would it take before *fawfaws* took the shape of stories of everyday Parisian life, stories in which I could play a part?

Desperate to be liked and accepted, I developed the skill of feigning understanding—nodding and smiling, parroting the speaker's expressions. It was especially effective for those chance encounters by the mailboxes in my lobby. It allowed me to build my reputation as a polite neighbor, and afforded me a connection du moment. But it left me feeling empty.

I was missing out on a chance to really meet people, marginalized by my inability to express who I was. I couldn't bring myself to open my mouth, and when I did, I sounded like a four-year-old. Yes. I like that. That is good. As a writer, I found not being able to express every subtle nuance of my thoughts exactly as I wanted was a kind of hell.

Oh, the dreaded moment when someone approached me and, smiling and full of expectation, said something, then, inevitably, found their words met by my dumb, glazed-over look. Their disappointment, palpable—and for me, gutting. I avoided eye contact with people because I didn't want them to engage me. That was my worst nightmare. Would I understand them? And if I did, could I reply?

At the market, while I was shopping for cheese at the fromager, an elegant man with thick, curly brown hair smiled at me. I smiled back but then realized I'd just engaged him. Oh dear God, don't talk to me, don't talk to me! I buried my head in the cheese.

"Fawfaw delicious, yes?" he asked, eyeing the cheese in my hand.

Not quite sure what he'd just said, I applied my trusty nod-and-smile technique.

His clear blue eyes smiled back. I wasn't sure how far I could fake it, but I sure wanted to try to go all the way with my charming suitor.

"For me," he said, pointing to another goat cheese, "I prefer faw fawfaw."

Okay, not terrible so far. I managed to glean that he was talking about the cheese, and that the particular goat cheese he'd referred to was better than the one in my hand.

"Yes? It's better?" I asked in my toddler French.

"I prefer it, yes. Faw faw very creamy fawfaw faw with fig preserves."

Very creamy. Fig preserves. Well, those words sounded delicious, so I took a risk. "Mmm," I said, hoping I got it right.

Thankfully, he smiled. Then he launched into what I could only suppose was a dissertation on the little-known wonders of goat cheeses and the different varieties across the country. I could make out *terroir*, a word describing the qualities of a region that give something its particular characteristics. But the rest came at me so fast and slurred together that I couldn't make out whole thoughts. I was swimming hard against the tide. Just when I'd figured out one word, ten more would fly by. Hard as I tried, I ended up drowning in a sea of *fawfaws*.

I felt my smile stiffen at the corners, and I was no longer nodding, frozen in *terroir*.

He paused mid-faw, and cocked his head. "You don't agree?"

Agree? Agree with *what*? My face flooded with warmth. *Abort! Abort!*

"I'm so sorry," I said in French, with the sweetest smile I could manage. "I don't speak French very well." I added round puppy eyes to soften the blow.

And there it was, that look of disappointment in those blue eyes. "Oh."

We stood there by the cheese, shrouded in a heavy, awkward silence. I understood his body language perfectly: door closed.

He smiled again, but it didn't light up his face this time. "No big deal," he said—*pas grave*. "Have a nice day."

But it was *grave*. It was very *grave*. The beautiful man was walking away from me. If I could just have understood him, spoken his language, he might have liked me, invited me for a coffee. That would have led to a date, then more dates, then a relationship—my God! I'd just driven away my French husband.

Because I couldn't carry on a conversation in French, this man would never learn that I was worth knowing. In English, I can be charming, witty, sophisticated. The life of the party, even. In French, I come off quiet, reserved, or, worse, dull. Paris Lisa was a pale imitation of the real thing, and unless I could speak their language well, the locals would never really know me.

But was my French the problem? Or was something else holding me back?

Putting myself out there—vulnerable, flawed—has been my greatest fear in life, and avoiding it, my life's work. I've always made sure before I said a thing or did a thing that I was knowledgeable or proficient. My fear of humiliation and ridicule borders on the pathological, part of me still that child doing whatever she can to please—to stay under the radar. Growing up, criticism was Ma's way of coaching, correcting—and bursting bubbles. Perfection, the only way to avoid the "ugly" mirror.

But it was my sister's criticism that may have had the most lasting effect. When we were kids, she had a knack for shoving me under the spotlight of shame, probably to deflect it from herself. The second I flubbed up, she'd be right there, pointing and laughing, calling me Dork.

So I learned that the best way to silence your critics was to do everything better than they did. And if that wasn't possible, not to participate at all.

This was probably why I still hadn't sent my novel to prospective agents, or why I hadn't gone for that opera career even after twelve years of training. Not perfect enough.

Or was I not worthy enough? Was perfection my excuse, another way of keeping myself safely tucked away? Was I still that little girl in her room, hiding from the world?

If I was going to live here in Paris, I'd need to get over it and put myself out there—participate whether I had the skills or not. That meant saying the wrong word, using the wrong verb tense, generally getting it wrong most of the time. Yes, people might laugh, but if I was going to connect, really connect, I'd have to learn to be okay with being a dork.

I wanted to be more like Geoffrey, someone who has no problem putting himself out there, way out there. He insists on speaking English to me—"Eet's more cool"—in spite of the fact that his knowledge of the language is limited, maybe slightly better than my French. No matter. English, or something like it, flies out of his mouth at lightning speed. Verb conjugations? Tenses? Who cares? If he doesn't know the word, he just Anglicizes a French word and keeps moving along. "Day" becomes "journey," from the French word journée, meaning the entire duration of the day. He'll regale us with tales of "zuh crazy journey I 'ad today."

When Geoffrey plans, he "planifies," because by his way of speaking, that's how you make a "planification."

He also has his own unique way of saying of my name, Lisa: for Geoffrey, it's Liza, with a long i and a zee sound. Oh, you mean that's not how all Americans say it? Too late. I am now Liza to my Paris friends.

We call these little peccadillos Geoffrey-isms.

My friend's ability to repurpose his limited English vocabulary is inspiring. It's poetry the way he strings a thought together, inventing new ways to express his emotions, and his thick accent only adds to his "isms."

"Oh my God, Liza!" he said over dinner one evening, breathless over something remarkable he'd seen. "My hass was out of my 'ead!"

Huh? "Your ass?"

"Yes! My hass was out of my 'ead!"

Wow, it must have been something incredible, to have turned him inside out like that. But, my, don't these French have some colorful expressions? "Wait a minute—did you say your 'ass' was out of your head?" I patted the corresponding region on my own body.

"No!" He pointed to his face. "Hass! Hass!"

"Oh! Eyes!"

We laughed until tears came out of our "hass."

That's how the expression "My ass was out of my head" became a permanent part of our vocabulary.

As flawed as Geoffrey's English is, he doesn't let it hold him back. He makes himself not only understood, but *felt*. No matter what he's saying, the real Geoffrey shines through, probably *because* of the flaws.

Did I have the guts to be flawed like that?

My contractor's carpenter, a New Zealander named Josh, puttered around my apartment, finishing up small projects left over from the big renovation. Two days of work had become five, and I'd taken to calling him Eldin, after the omnipresent handyman in the television series *Murphy Brown*. I shared my entire first stay in my apartment with him. Like Eldin and Murphy, we'd chat over tea each morning, or discuss current events while he painted trim or installed a new lock.

"Hey, Lisa," he asked as I was leaving the apartment to shop home décor, "you going to Castorama again?"

"Uh, *why?*" I knew what was coming. He'd already had me pick up a brass plate for the door while I was at Bazar de l'Hôtel de Ville the day before, and a can of trim paint the day before that. I didn't mind doing it; it was actually a lot of fun working on my own apartment, putting on the finishing touches.

"If you want me to hang your mirror, I need some wall anchors," he said.

I eyed the huge tool kit he would thunk onto my living room floor each day. "You don't have wall anchors anywhere in there?"

He shook his head. "Not big enough to handle the weight of *that* mirror." He was referring to the nineteenth-century Napoléon III mirror I'd just bought at the Marché au Puces de Saint-Ouen, an enormous flea market in the north of the city. It was four feet tall and crowned with a laurel wreath design that added another eight inches to its height.

Josh drew a picture of what he needed and wrote down the word in French: *cheville*. "Make sure it can handle up to fifty kilos."

"Yes, boss." I examined his strangely phallic rendition of the item. "Not sure how helpful this sketch is going to be."

He reexamined his drawing, shrugged. "Just ask the guy for a 'she-VEE-yuh,'" he said, enunciating as if for a child. "You'll be fine."

I'm not asking anybody for anything, I promised myself. That's the beauty of Castorama, a megastore near Place de la Nation where you can find everything from home décor to full kitchens. In a store as big as that one, I'd be assured the security of anonymity.

I found the *cheville* on my own quite easily, thank you, along with a few other things I didn't know I needed, such as taupe hand towels for the bathroom and a pack of nifty chamois dusting cloths I couldn't have lived without. I also figured, while I was in the store, I'd pick up a tape measure.

Yet, after combing through all three floors of the store, a tape measure eluded me.

It looked like I would be forced to—God help me—"ask the guy." What was the French word for "tape measure" anyway?

The staff at this megastore are buff twenty-something men who stand around in their tight-fitting uniforms just waiting for you to approach them. If this were New York, I'd come to this store weekly just to ask these hotties for stuff I didn't need, but here in France, they were terrifying.

I inched up to the most sympathetic-looking of the hot salesmen and, in my best bad French, attempted to ask for a thing when I didn't know the name for the thing.

"Oh, hello there. I'm looking for a tool used to measure things, but silly me, I don't know what it's called in French" was what I *wanted* to say. What came out was, "Good day. I am looking for a useful for to make the measure but I am not sure the word."

The hot man's face tightened as if his mind were tugging on it, working hard to comprehend. He leaned in closer, and my heart pounded—but for all the wrong reasons.

Holy crap, what do I do now?

If I left the store without that tape measure, I'd never forgive myself, so I flashed the man a big smile and pantomimed pulling a tape measure out—Zzzip!—then laying it down on something. *Tac!*

I was quite proud of my flawless use of the French expression *tac!*

The man's eyes widened, and a huge smile of relief came over his face. "Ah, un *mètre!*"

Yes! Eureka! We'd understood each other. *Youpi!* as the French say.

He then explained where the tape measures could be found, and it all went pear shaped again. Oh well. More pointing and pantomiming, and I finally left there with my tape measure.

I should have felt like a dork—hadn't that been my worst fear?—but instead, the experience left me exhilarated. I'd connected to that salesman and got what I needed. I'd *communicated*—to that really hot salesman.

I wondered what else Josh might need tomorrow. I suddenly liked being his errand girl.

Emboldened by my successful foray into hardware, I dropped a little French here and there, introduced myself to the owners of the local businesses I frequented, and attempted real small talk with my neighbors in the lobby of our building, instead of just nodding to them.

I asked my friends to arm me with phrases I'd need for my errands and ventured out farther still. At the cheese shop, I told the shopkeeper I was having a *cocktail dinatoire* and would he help me choose some cheese—cow, goat, and sheep. Except I forgot the word for sheep. Instead of panicking, I just bleated. He got the point. And, yes, he laughed—but not *at* me. This was a joke we shared.

Once I got over my paralyzing fear of humiliation, and opened myself up to people, I realized that, in my neighborhood, where no tourists ventured and few Americans lived, I was a novelty. My neighbors seemed charmed by my awkward attempts to explain myself. They'd pitch in and help me get to the point. After all, since they couldn't speak English, in this battle to comprehend one another, we were in this together.

I was starting to put myself out there, into strange new territory, but at least the natives were friendly.

· Seven ·

Eating Paris

Hot, crusty bread slathered with Brittany butter flecked with chunks of sea salt? Fudgy chocolate squares, called *pavés*, that stick to the roof of your mouth where they melt slowly? Foie gras and truffle sandwiches? Come on, Paris, that's not fair.

Now that I was making regular trips to Paris, I was noticing how the city conspired to sabotage my figure. The shop windows enticed with glorious displays, the pastries presented as if they were jewels in the window at Harry Winston. Even the humblest shops in working-class neighborhoods like mine took pride in every tart, every piece of cheese, wrapping it up for you in elaborate paper packaging like origami.

How could a person say no?

Just a few minutes' walk from my apartment, a *patisserie* touted as one of the best in the city makes museum-worthy pastries, some even painted in gold. My favorite quickly became its *tarte au citron*—carved perfectly square, the lemon cream piped into rows of sunny yellow balls, like an abacus on which you can count the calories you're consuming. One ball: two hundred sit-ups. Six: a day at the gym. Luckily, there is a single serving size of just four balls. I could burn that off with a day of shopping, no doubt, and I'd have to shop, because if I kept eating that tart, I was going to need bigger clothes. Still, there is something about eating a beautiful piece of food that makes a person feel the world is a perfect place. Nothing bad can happen while you're chewing.

When I was young, even through my teenage years, I often just poked at my food. "You eat like a bird!" Ma always said. She'd lament that she'd been cursed with two daughters instead of sons—not because she thought boys were better; it was only that daughters never ate the food she prepared. I did savor her food, though; still had my favorite dishes; and when we were around the table eating together, everything at home felt safe and right.

My appetite, for better or worse, has increased since those days, and Paris is never short on temptations. I have no idea how Parisian women stay thin, and I don't believe any of those books that have been written on the subject. I'm convinced they just smoke cigarettes and drink coffee, because if they were actually eating the food, there is no way they'd be a size two—but if that's the case, I feel sorry for them. I'd rather be fed and happy, and a dress size bigger, than say no to the heavenly morsels offered up in every corner of the city.

Starting with the bread: There must be a law in Paris about having a *boulangerie* every few streets, because they are impossible to avoid. Any attempts at a low-carb, gluten-free diet don't stand a chance in this city. Crusty loaves piled high in the window, flaky croissants and *pain au chocolat*—I always resign myself to being bloated during my Paris visits. Ever since I was a baby, I've loved anything of the starch variety. According to my mother, it was all she could get me to eat. She used every trick, she'd tell me later, including the tried-and-true technique of front-loading a spoonful of carrots with applesauce. It had worked with my sister, but I would not be fooled. Exasperated, she threw half a bagel on the tray of my highchair. "Here, eat *that*!" Ma said I loved it, and "gummed" half of it before I'd had my fill. Bread has been my downfall ever since.

When I bought my place, I was told there was a *boulangerie* in the 10th arrondissement worth going out of the way for. They made an eggy brioche loaf called *mouna*, with a hint of orange flower water in the dough and a sweet, crunchy coating of pearl sugar on top. Toasted and buttered for breakfast—there was no better way to start a day than with that chewy, comforting mouthful.

When I'm in Paris, it is impossible not to think of food all day long. The neighborhood is full of *traiteurs* serving prepared dishes and specialty foods. Several stand side by side, just up the boulevard from my apartment. The *fromagerie*, or cheese shop, sits beside the Nicolas wine shop, followed by the gourmet chocolate shop, and the charcuterie, or deli. The aroma of each announces the wares long before you can read a single sign. At the *boucherie-rôtisserie*, golden roasted chickens rotate in unison on spits all day long, their buttery juices dripping onto a tray below, where potatoes lie, caramelized into crispy perfection and almost as good as Ma's. But you have to grab a bird early, because by six in the evening, they're all snatched up for the Parisians' dinners.

There's a reason Paris is known for its food, and I was on a mission to eat my way through the entire city, trip by trip. Each time I came, I'd have a short list of places I wanted to try, as if by eating Paris, I'd become more Parisian. Some of the hottest restaurants were cropping up in my new arrondissement, opened by young chefs who were shaking things up, reinventing the cuisine that Escoffier had defined in the early 1900s. These were buzz-worthy restaurants, but impossible to get into, often booked six months out, unless you were a VIP. But I'd had my fill of that in New York. Sure, those new places were probably amazing, but this was Paris, damn it—land of old bistros and brasseries, with their white tablecloths and wood-paneled walls, places that evoked the spirit of Paris the most. Those were the spots for me.

These venerable old eateries were disappearing, so they had to be relished, the ambiance lapped up every bit as much as the food. Many of the grandest brasseries had been in business over a hundred years—Art Nouveau palaces such as Bofinger and La Fermette

Marbeuf, dripping in gold molding and often with elaborate murals and stained-glass skylights. Just sitting in one of these restaurants transported you out of your humdrum life. Touristy? Yes, somewhat. But who cared?

Some old places cater to the locals, though, such as the bistro on nearby rue Paul Bert. Warm and friendly, it has a zinc-top bar and bent-wood chairs, the full monty of quintessential bistro charm. The owners offer a three-course prix fixe, or *le menu*, as it's called in France, that is relatively cheap, considering you roll out of there afterward promising to fast the next day. This is not a place for vegetarians, serving dishes such as a side of beef, rare, with *sauce Béarnaise*, a rustic pork terrine, and pigeon with foie gras. They do have an egg dish, served with huge slices of black truffle, that might pass for vegetarian, if the ingredients in the creamy sauce they lavish on it can be confirmed.

How vegetarians cope in Paris is a mystery—and it has to be a hopeless situation for vegans. Every menu seems to be meat with a side of meat on a bed of meat. The vegetables are often merely a garnish, or stewed beyond recognition and drowned in butter or vinaigrette. Salads are no better. Not a leaf of kale or even romaine makes it to your plate. The official lettuce of Paris is a buttery, fiber-free variety, over which are piled things such as roasted potatoes and *lardons*, cubes of pork fat. Delicious, yes. Healthy? Only for the soul. But that's the point, *non?*

My sister, a health coach and raw foods chef, but also a foodie, found herself at a moral crossroads when we came to Paris together the Christmas after our mother died. Even though she knew better, Maria couldn't resist the cheese and bread, the meat smothered in sauces. She complained afterward—she was bloated, she had a headache, she felt sluggish. Why, oh, *why* had she done it? She'd swear that the next day would be a healthier one, and then she'd do the same thing all over again.

How could she not? If you love food, Paris is your pusher, tempting you with buttery, fatty, yeasty goodness. You're helpless.

"Please," my sister begged me after five days, "can we go somewhere that serves something *different?*" Different? This was Paris, sister dear. Parisians like things the way they like things, and have been liking those things exactly that way for generations. *Different* is not a welcome word, much like *new*. To do things differently is subversive thinking devised to undermine the rich traditions that have made Paris Parisian.

And of course, it's precisely those things that expats and visitors love about the city.

The cafés are the most Parisian part of Paris, where most Parisians can be found, especially just before dinner, having a drink, or the *apéro*. The food at most cafés is pretty average, often flash-frozen and uninspired, standard fare such as *croque monsieur*: toasted or grilled ham and cheese on a sweet brioche called *pain de mie* and dressed with a creamy béchamel, or Mornay sauce. Top it with a fried egg, and you have the *croque madame*. Both are meant to be eaten with a knife and fork, as is the other café staple: *le hamburger*. But when I'd see someone preciously slicing his or her burger into bite-size bits, it made the skin on the back of my American neck tighten.

Other café menu regulars: *poulet rôti*, or roasted chicken; *steak frites*, usually ribeye or skirt steak served with fries. And on the lighter side, *la salade composée*, a salad where each element is organized in some decorative manner, necessitating that you toss them together yourself, which can be a challenge on a tiny café table. Choice of dressing for your salad? Please, this is France; you'll eat what they serve—and it is always creamy Dijon mustard. Always. The same creamy Dijon dressing at every café across all of Paris. The only place "French" dressing exists is in the United States.

But then, you don't go to the cafés for the food. In a city of minuscule apartments, people use the café as their living room, office, reading room. You can stay as long as you want, and many cafés have free WiFi, or *weefee*, as the French pronounce it. I was happy to sit in one all day, even on my short stays. At a café on Canal

Saint-Martin, I sat for five hours, as various friends came and went, writing and watching the people, and the barges, go by. No one tried to hustle me out in order to turn over the table. This wasn't New York; this was the land of the *flâneur*: he who takes the time to take life in. In Paris, to sit and watch the world go by over a glass of wine or a cup of coffee is not a luxury; it is an essential part of a happy life.

Up the boulevard from my new apartment, one café quickly became my HQ where I'd meet friends for drinks or dinner—or I'd write. I'd often see the same people at the same time of day doing likewise. In a country where food is an inherent part of the culture, it made sense that the café would be the center of Parisian daily life. This alone could be why I loved Paris so much, since food was such a central part of my life growing up. Sitting at a table all day long, watching the world go by, surrounded by people enjoying their food and their friends—this made for a richer life.

Bouillon Chartier, in the 9th arrondissement, has been in business since 1896. If Fabien hadn't taken me there, I wouldn't have known it existed.

"I cannot believe you 'ave never been!" Bouillon Chartier's draw, Fabien told me, besides its history, was that it served good food at ridiculously low prices. A *bouillon*, he told me, is a kind of *cantine* or, more literally, "soup hall."

You could spot the place as soon as you turned the corner on rue du Faubourg-Montmartre—from the neon arrow pointing out its location and the long queue of tourists outside.

I accused Fabien of taking me to a tourist trap. Didn't he know me by now?

"Parisians come here, too," he said, undaunted by my eye rolling. "You will see."

Fabien's father used to take him to Chartier as a boy. As he described those meals he'd shared with his father—a man with whom things have since become strained—he looked off, his eyes focusing on nothing in particular. "It's very special here," he said. His lips curled into a smile.

Fabien hadn't just taken me to a restaurant; he'd invited me into his past. Chartier was to him what Anderson's Frozen Custard in Buffalo is to me. A landmark, Anderson's original drive-in from the early 1950s is just a block away from my aunt Mary's house. They serve a Buffalo classic called beef on weck, a roast beef sandwich served au jus with horseradish on a German-style roll called kemmelweck, but they are really known for their soft frozen custard.

When we were kids, visiting from New Jersey during the summers, my sister and I were allowed to walk there for custard with the boys who lived next door. To us, Buffalo was "the big city." Even my aunt's suburb of Kenmore was exciting to us kids: you could hear sirens and see the lights of downtown on the horizon. In New Jersey, we were living in bleak tract housing surrounded by cornfields and not much else. When my grandmother visited us in New Jersey for the first time, she marveled in her thickly accented English, "But you got-a white-a dust 'ere in the *campagne!*" In industrialized Buffalo, she was used to vacuuming up black factory soot.

Out in the "country" as Gramma called it, the ice-cream truck came to us. In Buffalo, to be able to walk to Anderson's on our own was independence. Sometimes we'd stop at the train tracks to put a penny on the rail and wait for a train to pass over it. This was the best part of the walk. The train rushing by would blow our sundresses back, send our ponytails whipping around. We'd have to search for the penny afterward. When I was clearing out Ma's house, I found one of those flattened and stretched pennies in the dresser drawer of my childhood bedroom.

The train line has long been shut down, but the Anderson's on Sheridan Drive, near my aunt's house, still serves my favorite chocolate and vanilla "twist" on a cake cone. I can count on Anderson's to be there, even though my aunt is gone; my Ma, too. It connects me to my past in a visceral way. Keeps me eternal somehow.

Anderson's is part of my story. Chartier is part of Fabien's, and while inside its walls, he can still connect with his father.

How could I not love this place, too? Tourists and all?

We didn't have to wait long to enter the restaurant. The line, though at least a hundred deep, moved surprisingly fast. We were swept through the door in just under ten minutes. Once inside, I understood why.

Fabien was right to call it a "hall." It was cavernous, as wide as it was high—two stories tall. Tables and booths filled every square inch of the floor with additional tables on a mezzanine level. It looked as if a thousand people could be served here. Dozens of waiters in black vests and long white aprons dashed around the room. The din of the diners made my ears ring.

Large mirrors were set into the ornate paneled walls of cream on white. A skylight spanned the entire ceiling and, suspended from it, turn-of-the-century globe lamps gave off light that screamed off the mirrors and white walls, making me squint. A giant clock hung on the back wall, the only thing in the room that reminded me that time was indeed *not* standing still, unlike the interior, which looked as if it hadn't been touched in over a hundred years—the brass luggage racks over the booths still intact since the days when this was part of a train station concourse, Fabien explained, as was the giant clock. Wooden tables with cast-iron bases were dressed in red-and-white check tablecloths, as they had always been, each topped with a large sheet of white paper.

Almost too cliché, but it sucked you in all the same.

We were taken to a table for four against a wall just under the mezzanine stairs—a cozy nook all our own. Except we'd be sharing it. At the table, an English couple was working through their main course. This was not a place that stood on ceremony.

The menu was printed on a single sheet of paper, two-sided,

from what looked like the same printing plates they'd used since the 1920s. The prices looked like it, too. Fabien had to confirm what I was reading. Appetizers for a buck eighty? Half a carafe of wine for *seven* euros?

"Yes!" he said. "That's what I tell you!"

You could see why this place had a long tradition of drawing working-class Parisians. Here, they served decent, honest food at low prices.

Our waiter whizzed toward us as soon as we were settled: a middle-aged man whose agile body negotiated the tightly packed tables with the grace and athleticism of a figure skater, his hips swiveling from side to side, a tray held aloft, balanced on the fingertips of one hand, effortlessly, as though he'd worked here since he was fourteen. And he probably had. He was gruff but smiling.

"Je vous écoute!" he said. *I'm listening to you!*

For me: roasted chicken and fries, a small carafe of burgundy; Fabien: three vegetarian appetizers—another reason he loved this place. The waiter scribbled down our order directly on the paper covering our table, then glided off again.

The English couple left. Their plates were whisked away, a clean paper table cover was slapped over the cloth, two new place settings added. Another couple, Parisians, joined us at the table.

This place was a well-oiled machine, a giant food factory—move 'em in, feed 'em, move 'em out. Plates sailed out of the kitchen, carried over our heads by the sea of waiters who served them to an ever-rotating crowd of hungry, happy people eating, drinking, and laughing. Even if the food was only so-so, it was well worth coming here just for the spectacle.

The food was as promised. Like Anderson's beef on weck, not spectacular but totally satisfying. It was about more than the food anyway.

After we finished, our waiter jotted down prices beside the order he'd written on our table cover, and tallied them in seconds.

The entire meal—four appetizers, one main dish, half a carafe of wine, two desserts, and coffee—cost thirty-five euros.

"I was right?" Fabien asked. "You like Chartier?"

I nodded. There was nothing pretentious about the place, nothing contrived, and it had memories tucked into every corner. A piece of history that was still a vital part of the city—like Anderson's is to Buffalo—keeping time standing still just long enough for a person to get his bearings, to feel safe in the spinning world. Inside the walls of Chartier with Fabien, I felt as if everything was a little more okay, as if a small part of the wound left by my mother's passing might be healing over just by my sitting here at this table in the corner of this big old soup hall.

· Eight ·

Le Dating Game

It's easier to meet men in Paris than New York. French men are more forward, for starters. They make eye contact with you on the street—real, lingering eye contact, not the New York side glance that says, "I'm afraid you'll call me a pervert for checking you out." Parisian men *want* you to know they appreciate the sight of you. When I first encountered this, I walked around blushing all day. This level of connection with a stranger was foreign to me, certainly when you're just going about your business from point A to point B.

"Charmante," they'd say. *Charming.*

It wasn't leering or lusty. No one was giving the "hey, baby." It was a grown-up, sophisticated flirtation between two people that was honest, and surprisingly personal.

Men engaged me in conversation everywhere, from the grocery store to the Métro platform. Young men, too—like *twenty.* I'm no old lady, but the last time a twenty-year-old hit on me in New York, Guns N' Roses was on the charts.

Paris was really good for my ego.

Meeting French men was the easy part. Dating them was where things got complicated.

I'd had some very romantic dates in Paris—with guys who

really made an effort to make a woman feel special. One man was the manager of a restaurant I'd been at one night. We'd had a connection, and he took me out a few times. Our first date was lunch on a rainy Sunday. We dined in an intimate bistro with dark paneled walls in Saint-Germain-des-Prés, talked for hours at our cozy table by the fireplace. Then we walked along the Seine under an umbrella together.

On our second date, he picked me up in his car after his shift, and we toured the city lights, finishing the night in Montmartre, looking out over the rooftops until the sun began to rise. He was such a gentleman—only cheek kisses and hand holding—a real old-fashioned courtship. He wrote me eagerly once I was back in New York, seemed game to make something happen, but his letters tapered off after a while, then disappeared. My last "How are you?" email went unanswered. Maybe he'd found a woman closer to home.

Another man I met planned a whole day for our first date. He wanted to show me all the things I'd never seen in Paris, including a visit to the top of the Eiffel Tower. It was touching that he made such an effort. A charming and genuine gesture. He also pursued me when I was back in New York. We made plans to see each other again, on my next trip to Paris, but when the date came he stood me up, even though I had his email from the prior week confirming. Was it something I'd done? Or hadn't done?

One might have thought it was a Parisian thing to run hot and cold, but there were plenty who ran only hot—too hot for me. These were the persistent ones, the ones who called over and over until I picked up. If I didn't answer right away, they'd call right back a minute later. I met a man who called me ten times in three minutes. I was having dinner in a noisy restaurant and didn't hear the phone. It seemed absurd, so I texted him to see if he was "butt-dialing" me. He wasn't; he just really, really, *really* wanted to see me. Really? Where I come from, that's called stalking. In Paris, it's completely acceptable.

Was Paris the City of Codependent Love?

My experiences were echoed by my female expat friends, most of whom had been at it longer than I. Because Paris had become so familiar, I'd forgotten I was dealing with a different culture. There was a lot to learn about dating here.

I'd been laboring under the misapprehension that the French had a sophisticated view of dating and love—modern, open, and free, à la Simone de Beauvoir and Jean-Paul Sartre. It was an innocent mistake. In fact, the dating rituals in France are actually much more provincial than I'd expected and, to a New Yorker, downright naïve.

The idea of the casual date didn't really exist, or so I was told. Everyone seemed to be looking for love. That could explain why they came on so strong with the heavy-handed romance. It also may be the reason some of the men bailed on me after one or two dates. Why invest in me if I'm not going to be around for another eight weeks? A man could meet a whole bunch of women in that time.

No casual dating meant it wasn't really acceptable to date more than one man at a time, at least not with him knowing about it. So, no dating around until you found Monsieur Right. One date was supposed to lead to two, then three, then—*voilà!*—you were a couple.

I'd also learned you shouldn't kiss a man on the mouth on the first date—unless you wanted to sleep with him. So, was this why the men I dated were so physically reserved with me? Had it been up to *me* to make the first move? Perhaps this was the reason the verb *baiser* no longer meant "to kiss," but "to have sex" in the modern vernacular. You really had to be careful dating in Paris. Whether saying it or doing it, this kiss was tricky business.

If you did want to sleep with a guy you were dating, you'd better be ready for a relationship, because after you had sex, you were going steady.

It was like high school.

In 1955.

Based on what I was learning, if I had wanted one of those nice men who'd taken me on the romantic dates to stick around, I should have staked my claim, planted that kiss, and used sex to snag him.

That didn't seem terribly modern to me. Or even terribly adult.

The word *love* got tossed around easily and early by men. It was hard to take seriously. If it were that easy to fall in love, how real could it be? Maybe I was a jaded New Yorker, but this was a country where the verb for "to like" and "to love" was the same, *aimer*, so I couldn't help but be suspicious. Why the big hurry, guys? Afraid someone else would snatch me up? Why did I have to commit to someone after just a few dates? Wasn't that hasty? Or desperate?

Maybe the point isn't romance, or even sex. Maybe Parisians just long to be *attached*. The ones I know went from one committed relationship to another, and had only a handful of relationships in their adult lives. It's great if you're looking for a Frenchman to settle down with. A few of my expat friends met their Parisian husbands within the first few months of living in Paris. Met a guy, had some dates—and *bam*! Got married. And they're all still together, so there's something to be said about the Parisian dating ritual.

Except I wasn't looking for marriage, or even a heavy committed relationship. I was just dipping my toe into the waters of Parisian life. I wasn't ready to take the plunge.

On one of my visits, an expat friend and her French husband invited me to what I can only describe as an intervention masked as brunch in Montmartre. It started out harmlessly enough, but quickly became an intense discussion about me and my single status, which seemed to be a deficiency of some kind. I was missing out on the marvels of being in a couple. "You're an incredible woman," my friend said. "We just want to see you happy in a relationship."

Wasn't it possible to be an incredible *single* woman? Was all this unhitched fabulousness some sort of threat to couples everywhere? Or was being single—what?—a disease needing a cure?

I felt cornered suddenly, violated even. Would it be rude if I walked out? Because this was seriously screwed up.

"It's fine for you," I said. "But not every woman wants to be married."

"Not *married*, necessarily." My friend smiled sweetly, her eyes pleading with me to understand how much happier I could be. "Wouldn't it be nice to have someone to share your life with?"

How about no? How's no for an answer?

This was the first time in my life I didn't have to worry about anyone but myself. Hadn't I earned the right to enjoy this blissful solitude—to steep in it, as if it were a hot tub at a spa, until my fingers were pruney? I was just starting to feel strong again; the last thing in the world I needed was for some guy to mess that up.

But, of course, since my friend had found lasting love, she wanted the same for me. She met her husband pretty quickly after arriving in Paris, but she had been looking for love. While she'd spent a long time being single before she met her husband, I'd spent those same years in and out of relationships. A few were long-term, committed ones, rough rides that shook me up badly. The last one gave me such a walloping that I was still licking my wounds five years later. I wanted a break.

So, I hadn't come to Paris looking for love; I was still building a life without Ma and needed to figure it all out before I let anyone in. I was a gaping wound; I didn't want to inflict myself on someone else right now. Sure, there were flirtations with men since I'd been coming here, possibilities of something more, but nothing had materialized because I was in a period of transition, and as we all know, it's hard for Cupid to hit a moving target.

That's what I'd been telling myself, but I knew the truth: I'd been much happier out of relationships than in—a more stable, even-keeled person. I preferred the single version of myself much more than that spineless pushover I became when I was in love. *Oh, yes, sweetie, you're right; it was my fault. Are you okay? Are you sure you're okay?* Where would I have learned to be anything but a codependent mate, the fixer growing up in a home where I'd convinced myself that everyone else's happiness, especially Ma's, was something I could control?

Relationships were bottomless pits of need swallowing me up. I'd given away pieces of myself with each one. After years of inviting chaos and abuse, over and over, I had no faith in my ability to choose the right mate. So I just didn't get in the dating game.

My mother never liked any of the men I brought home. Flat out *hated* most of them. And she wasn't the sort of woman to mince words, so the boyfriend knew it, too. Looking back, in some cases—probably in most cases—I see that Ma was right about the man, but at the time, she made life hell. It wasn't completely about the man for her; it had a lot more to do with a competition between her and the man for my attention. She'd still have found fault with the perfect man, if I'd ever found him, still have tried to drive a wedge between us.

"Oh, I suppose I'll never see you now," Ma would say when I started dating a new guy, and I knew how it would play out from there: a tug of war between her and the boyfriend, with me in the middle, stretched to the breaking point.

The worst time was after Dad died. I met someone two months later, which was much too soon, in Ma's view: a good daughter would have devoted all her energies to her grieving mother. It didn't help that my boyfriend was equally manipulative and equally possessive of my time. My breakdown came one night when Ma was on the phone haranguing me about not being there for her, and he was saying nearly the same thing in my other ear.

Later in her life, Ma lamented the fact I hadn't married or given her grandchildren. I asked her, "What did you do to encourage me or foster that?"

The sad part is she'd have been an amazing grandmother, just watching how she was with my friends' kids. She could be so generous, funny, loving. But her insecurity—and my need to please—wrote the story we both wanted least: me alone, and she with no legacy.

Was Ma the reason I'd never married up to now? At some point we're responsible for our own choices, aren't we? According to my therapist—whom I started seeing after that breakdown the day my mother and boyfriend pushed me over the edge—the reason I kept dating the wrong guy was because I was trying to work through the bigger issue: that would be Ma. Instead of working it out in therapy and learning to have a healthy relationship, I had made Ma an even bigger part of my life, leaving little room for anyone else. I stopped bringing guys home to meet her. Then, at some point, I just stopped having serious relationships altogether.

But what about now that she was gone? I'd bought the apartment in Paris; was I subconsciously making room in my life for more? Or was it enough just to take care of myself for now? That was probably the relationship I'd neglected the most, the one needing the most work.

Nine

Home Sweet Homes

Rush hour, Rockefeller Center subway station, New York. I reached into my coat pocket and pulled out two objects: my New York subway MetroCard and a ticket for the Paris Métro. People whizzed all around as I stood wondering which one to use. Where was I?

Nearly a year after buying my apartment in Paris, I was averaging a visit every six to eight weeks. My job afforded four weeks' vacation, and I was eking them out in long weekends. Each time I arrived in Paris, opened the door of my little home, a rush would go through me. It still smelled of fresh paint, the dream world I'd built still new and surprising.

Before I had the apartment, I went to Paris twice a year, spring and fall, to write about the fashion trade shows for a Francophile website. It was an event I planned for months in advance—buying special outfits, exchanging dollars for euros, renting a French cell phone.

The rental phone, more than anything, represented my Paris relationship: temporary. The first thing I did when I landed in the city was program all my Parisian friends' numbers into the address book. Once back in New York, I'd have to erase them—and with them, my Paris life. I made a ceremony of it, saying, "See you next time," as I hit Delete All.

I lived a New York life punctuated by Paris.

This was changing. The space between my two cities seemed to be shrinking, because the time I spent away from Paris was shrinking, too. Just when I'd come back from Paris and get into my proverbial New York groove, it was time to turn around and go back to Paris again. A brief jet-lagged stay in Paris, and then back to New York. And back again.

It became a tradition to bookend my stays with parties: the welcome home party and the leaving party, or *fête de vidange*, as we called it, a play on the expression for grape harvest, *fête de vendange*— where we'd empty, or *vider*, my refrigerator before I'd close up the apartment and return to New York.

Always moving, I kept myself from dwelling on the loss I was still living with, and I knew if I stopped and thought about how huge my life had become, maybe more than I deserved, the Ma in my head—her fears and limitations still working away in there—might kibosh it. So I didn't stop. I just kept moving forward.

This revolving door life made me dizzy, blurring my cities together. I'd crave a restaurant in one city, then remember it was in the other. Search for my favorite red scarf only to realize afterward it was on the shelf an ocean away. And yes, for a brief second now and then, I'd forget which subway system I was riding.

Euro coins now jangled together in the bottom of my purse with their American cousins, clothes filled closets in both cities, and the address book in one phone brought all my friends together.

No more was my life divided, Paris vs. New York.

The biggest side effect of all this: Paris was no longer foreign. I didn't need time to adjust to it anymore; part of me was existing in both cities now, like a time traveler living two simultaneous realities connected by email, party plans, to-do lists.

I thought the apartment would just be like having my own

private hotel room—no more check-in times or heavy luggage—but its very existence changed my relationship with the city.

Usually, it's a profound event that creates a shift in a relationship, something remarkable you tell your grandkids about, but my connection to Paris was intensifying because of the humble, insignificant things. The more commonplace something became, the more it tugged me close. Shopping for groceries, grabbing a glass at happy hour with my friends, waving hello to the café owners—these everyday routines made me a part of Paris life in an intimate and real way.

I wasn't a visitor anymore.

My connection to Paris wasn't all that had shifted. Something in me had shifted, too. I was expanding as my world was.

My neighbors called me "the American." It wasn't said with distain, as in "What is that *American* doing in our building?" It was more of a wide-eyed "Are you the American?" That an American from New York had chosen their corner of the world seemed to tickle them. It tickled me to imagine my story circulating in the halls.

"*Bonjour*, Claire. Raining again."

"*Bonjour*, Charlotte. Yes, terrible rain this time of year. Did you hear an American moved into the building?"

"I did. Madame Hamidou told me she's from New York."

"New York! How glamorous. Have you seen her yet?"

"No, have you?"

"No."

And that was the problem. They'd never seen "the American" because she was hardly there. Her here-again, gone-again Paris life left everyone wanting, especially her. Just when I'd get my Paris life going, I'd have to put it on pause.

It didn't bother me in the beginning, but a year in, as my connection to the community intensified, I started to feel like I was missing out—because I was.

The apartment had started out as a diversion from grief, something to pick me up, but now I craved a deeper, more meaningful connection. A sense of belonging. Maybe I was still trying to fill the hole Ma's death had left, a hole that grew more profound with time, not less.

On one of my visits, my last evening of the trip, I met a new neighbor while climbing the stairs to my apartment—a man and his child. The little boy, maybe eighteen months old, was trying to walk up a step on his own, determined but shaky. Dad was right behind, patiently watching over in case his son toppled.

We greeted each other with a *Bonsoir*, and I started up the stairs, smiling at the baby as I passed. He reached out and gripped my long coat, using it to hoist himself up the step.

Helping him, I asked, "What are you doing, my little man?" *Mon petit homme.* This was the one time my toddler French worked for me.

The father smiled broadly, said something about the boy loving to climb, followed by some other words I didn't catch.

"So cute," I said in French. *Très mignon.*

"Ah, fawfaw, faw fawfaw!" the father responded.

Here we go again. "Pardon?"

The man scrutinized my face. "Are you the American?" *Êtes-vous l'américaine?*

Why, yes indeed, I was that non-French-speaking American lady. "New York."

"Ah, New York! I love it! I have a friend fawfawfaw! Welcome!"

I thanked him. "Nice to meet you."

"Nice to meet you. Ah, New York! Marvelous!"

We stood there nodding at each other, I having run out of French, and he knowing no English.

"Okay, see you later," I offered. *À bientôt.*

"Okay! See you later!"

We parted on the stairs, but five minutes later there was a timid knock on my door. It was the man, this time sans baby. "My wife and I would like to invite you to our place for a drink."

What? Wow. This was an invitation inside the private life of my neighbors, the ultimate stamp of approval—except . . . "Tonight? I have plans. I'm sorry." And I would be leaving the next day.

"No, no, not tonight, but another night. You will?"

I wanted to explain that I was leaving but would love to make a plan for when I was back, desperate to seize this rare opportunity. But my French let me down. "Yes! Thank you. So nice."

"Okay! Very good," my neighbor said. His eyes smiled warmly; his mouth was more reserved, only a tiny curl. "I will tell my wife. See you soon!"

"Yes, soon." But I knew it wouldn't be soon; it would be at least two months.

My lovely, hospitable neighbor probably came by a week later, maybe even tried a few times, knocking on the door of an empty apartment. Did they wonder what had happened to me? Had they given up and moved on?

Even after several more trips to Paris, I never ran into that neighbor again. The ship had sailed.

In fact, the building had a lot of tenant turnover, which was the case when you have few owners living in a building: most of the apartments were occupied by transient renters, many students or young couples who'd move on to something bigger after a baby was born. Maybe this is what had happened to my invitation to cocktails. It had moved farther out to the suburbs, where there was more space for entertaining.

There were only a few faces I saw regularly. One of them was my neighbor across the hall, Cyril, who was on the board of the co-op, or *conseil syndical*, with whom I'd attempt small talk. He knew enough English that we got on pretty well. I invited him and his partner to one of my soirées one night and he accepted enthusiastically but never showed. Perhaps we hadn't understood each other as well as I had thought?

There were also the two striking men who lived together in an apartment on an unknown floor above, with whom I'd shared only the friendly *bonjour* in the stairwell. I called them the Smith Brothers because they both had huge beards and reminded me of the two men pictured on the box of cough drops named for the famous bearded brothers. My bearded neighbors, not brothers yet very alike, were always dressed in perfectly tailored suits and highly polished shoes, their beards neatly trimmed. If I hadn't known they were also on the *conseil* with Cyril, I'd have sworn they were friendly ghosts from the 1880s who still roamed the halls and helloed everyone as they passed on the stairs. *Boooooo-jour!*

Andrea was my neighbor on the ground floor, the *rez-de-chaussée*, whom I'd met the first week I stayed in my apartment. The water shutoff valve had started to leak in my brand-new bathroom, and my contractor was nowhere to be found. I ran to the store to stock up on as many absorbent products as I could carry until a plumber could be called. But where would I get a plumber, and how would I communicate with said plumber? And would there even be one available in August, when everyone was on vacation?

"Ma, you gotta help me," I mumbled as I entered the lobby, a year's supply of paper towels and sponges in my arms. That's when I saw Andrea for the first time.

"Is there a concierge in the building?" I asked her in French, panicked.

"Je pense que non," she replied—*I think not*—but with a very Anglicized pronunciation. *Zjuh punce kuh noooo.*

Was she English, I asked? No, she was from Canada.

"I'm from Buffalo!" I chirped, as if it were the same thing. Well, it was sort of the same thing. All you had to do was drive over the Peace Bridge and you could have lunch in Canada, which we in Buffalo did, often.

"I went to the university in Buffalo!" she chirped back.

Then we chirpety-chirped for twenty minutes in the lobby. Andrea helped me call the managing agent and arrange for a plumber.

She even stayed with me until the plumber came, so she could play interpreter. But that's Canadians for you.

Andrea, as it turned out, lived not only in Buffalo, but on the same street where I lived until I was two years old. The same street, in the same town. My mother had to have arranged this meeting from heaven. How else could you explain an English-speaking neighbor who had lived in Buffalo on my old street, right here in my new apartment building just when I needed her?

Whatever the explanation, that Buffalo connection created an instant friendship. Andrea and I met nearly every day for happy hour at our local café after she got off work, and shopped together on Saturdays in the Bastille. In New York, most of my female friends had gotten married and moved to the suburbs; all I had left were my gay guy friends to pal around with, as if I were Judy Garland. I missed having a girlfriend to do girl things with. But here in Paris, I had Andrea, and she would help my home feel even homier.

Another neighbor I saw frequently was an elderly woman who lived on the floor below me. Everyone saw Isabella frequently; she was a fixture on the street, walking up and down every day despite needing a cane, visiting with the neighboring building's *gardienne*, or "lady superintendent." She never had a hair out of place, was always impeccably but simply put together, most often in slacks with a chic blazer and a lovely pin on her lapel. Just like Ma.

Originally from a wealthy family in Spain who lost it all during the Franco years, Isabella is highly educated and has lived in more than six countries, including the United States. She speaks Spanish, French, Polish, German, Italian, Portuguese, and a little English, but "Just a very leetle!" She plays piano and violin, and dances flamenco. You learn all this in great detail because once you have Isabella's ear, you give up at least twenty minutes of your day to her tales. They're pretty riveting if you're willing to listen.

Between Spanish, Italian, and French, we managed to communicate pretty well, both of us switching to another language when a word eluded us in one.

Fate brought Isabella and me together at the heavy door of our building. She was entering as I was leaving, and I was able to help her open it. Then she bent my ear for several minutes. After this happened again a few more times, I began to suspect it wasn't fate, but that she'd often wait at the door until someone, anyone, could help her open it, and dispel the loneliness of her day.

That's when I started to look out for her. When I was going to the market, I'd stop by her apartment and ask her if she needed anything. I helped her get things down from the top of her closet, carry her heavy bags up the stairs. I alerted the building's managing agent of a leak that was staining her ceiling. She'd been afraid to complain about it.

"I'm an old woman. It's fine."

"It's not fine, Isabella! It can't stay like that. I'm going to complain."

"My daughter told me not to make a fuss."

Isabella's daughter had stashed her eighty-nine-year-old mother in this one-room apartment in East Paris so she could carry on with her life elsewhere, unfettered.

Isabella needed a daughter. I had lost a mother. Maybe it was fate after all.

But I was in Isabella's life only a few days at a time. Did anyone else look after her when I was in New York? Maybe it was just that Isabella reminded me of Ma, or maybe it was her fragility and loneliness that touched me, but I became more uneasy about leaving her each time I had to go—and not just Isabella; my life here, too.

I was growing deeply attached to Paris, more invested in what was happening around me. There were people who depended on me, who wanted me to be a part of their lives.

Those flights to New York were starting to feel less like going home and more like leaving it.

Ten

Ringing in the New Me

"New Year, New You" is a favorite headline among the promotions my team created for the January issues of our magazines. You've seen them: "Start the New Year off right with these great ideas, brought to you by . . ." They were always the same: product showcases with tips about how you could make the New Year better than the year before.

The hype of hope for a better year was lost on me. Every New Year started off with promise, but usually lost its bloom by spring, so why get your expectations up? The year my mother was diagnosed with cancer was one of those years. And I kicked off the year she died by sitting at her bedside in Morristown Memorial Hospital. It was all downhill from there.

But the year to which we were about to bid adieu was different. This one *started* on a low—I was still working through grief—but month by month, as my frame of mind improved, so did the year. My part-time life in Paris lifted me up and kept me facing forward, and even when we sold our childhood home, what might have been a sad ending signaled a new phase of life that was liberating.

New Year, New You.

Looking back, I could see how far I'd come, and I wanted to celebrate New Year's Eve in the city responsible for my transformation.

My friends and I started planning months before, firing off messages to one another—who was coming, what the menu should be. I was hosting the party in my apartment, and each of us would bring something. Geoffrey coordinated our efforts, shooting out long lists in his own Franglais:

MENU REVEILLON JOUR DE L'AN
- Petits fours, tapenade, humous, rillettes of tuna: Lisa & Geoffrey
- Variety of chips and crackers: Andrea
- Rosbeef and patatoes: Christophe
- Smoked salmon with lemon and crème fraîche: Geoffrey
- Salade végétarienne: Fabien
- Cheeses and fruits: Lisa & Geoffrey
- Dessert and chocolates: Yann
- *REMEMBER FABIEN IS ALLERGIC TO CHEESES AND CHOCOLATE!
- Variety of macarons: Fabien
- Sodas and water: 2 Coca Zero, 2 or 3 variety of fruits juice, and 2 Perrier: Andrea
- Champagne, wine: Lisa & Geoffrey
- Bread: Geoffrey

That was for six people. Anyone who might think it was too much food has never been to one of my parties. Four times more food than the number of people? That way of thinking is just in my Italian blood.

My parents hosted a New Year's Eve party every year, and Ma put out a huge spread. If there were eight guests, she cooked for twenty; twelve guests, enough for fifty. That was Ma math. She prepared all week for the event. The dining room table would be covered with every kind of finger sandwich, spread, dip, or platter imaginable. She'd make her special-occasion foods, normally too expensive or "too much a pain in the ass" for any other reason: crab salad, stuffed mushrooms, liver pâté, and my childhood favorite, deviled eggs.

And that was just the food *before* midnight. After Dick Clark counted us down to the New Year, Ma put the homemade pizzas in the oven. At 12:10 A.M., the second feast began, and carried on until two or three in the morning.

It was my mother's food almost more than anything else that I missed. The realization that I'd never eat her food again hit me some months after she was gone, one night in my own kitchen while I was preparing my meager supper. Never again would I eat her crispy roasted chicken; her juicy, peppery meatballs; or those sweet, tender stuffed peppers we called "gold" and fought over. Never again could I just ring her for cooking advice, ask about a family recipe.

I sobbed right there over my stove contemplating how far "never again" spanned, how deep it went. How permanent it was. Understanding that I'd never eat another of Ma's meals created a longing more profound than anything I'd felt since she died.

When Ma was first diagnosed with cancer, during breakfast one morning while I was visiting, she suddenly looked hard at me, assessing something.

"Do you know how to make meatballs?" she asked.

I shook my head.

"Do you know how to make stuffed peppers?"

No, I didn't. And she was trying to tell me I'd better learn fast. This was when we both realized she might not make it.

The fact that she would die before imparting that precious knowledge was what bothered her most.

I never did learn how to make her meatballs, or her stuffed peppers, but she did teach me our family sauce recipe. At least I think she did:

"You start by browning the meat in the bottom of the pot—ground meat, if you're lazy—but if you want to do it right, you need chicken wings, plump spare ribs about the size of my thumb, and on special occasions, braciola. Not those horrible giant things they make in Little Italy, with parsley and crap in them! Nice little ones. Just pound the beef and put some Romano cheese and lots of black pepper, then roll them up. Easy. Then put all the meat and chicken wings into the pot to brown them.

"Now, if you're any kind of an *Abruzzese*, you have to use lard to brown the meat. And really brown it—nice and crusty. That's where the flavor comes from. The neighbors throw their meatballs in the sauce, raw. Horrible. That's no way to cook. And don't let me catch you putting in garlic or onions. That's not Gramma's sauce!

"When the meat is browned, take it out and scrape up all that good stuff, then stir in the tomato paste. Add a can of tomatoes—the puree, because the chopped has too much water!—and a sliver of red pepper. That's the secret. When you get the sauce boiling up good, put the meats back in and simmer.

"Cook the hell out of it until it's black.

"Serves eight—or since you eat like a bird, ten."

I'd try to get the measurements and quantities—how much salt and pepper, for example—but that was always futile. Like her mother before her, Ma "felt" her way through the process. And maybe if I'd spent any time making some of her dishes, I'd get the feel for it, too.

When I was looking for an apartment in Paris, a proper oven was very important to me, even though, as a single woman on the go, I can count the times I've used my oven in New York. Salads, omelets—that was my thing. But in Paris I had visions of whipping up a meal for a houseful, like Ma did. Christmas *chez moi*. Wouldn't that be something?

I was keen to create a new Christmas tradition for my sister because it was still the hardest holiday for us without Ma. Unbearable. For us, our mother embodied the holidays. Decorating her house took days, and she loved every minute of it, the Firestone Christmas albums blaring through the crackling speakers of the 1970s stereo she still used. Her Santa collection alone took an afternoon—over a hundred from all over the world, each with its provenance: the friend who had given it to her, the quaint gift shop where she'd bought it. Her daughters contributed their share to the collection over the years. Those Santas from her "girls" were her favorites, of course.

Though we were adults, at Christmas in Ma's house, we became children again. She still bought us matching Christmas pajamas, which we'd get on Christmas Eve. Gifts overflowed under the tree on Christmas morning. Ma insisted on keeping the traditions alive for us. Now the person at the center of those traditions was gone.

It finally made sense to me why people cried when they heard Christmas carols, why this could be the most depressing time of the year.

Since Ma died, I'd been going through the motions of decorating my house only because the notion of not having a tree felt worse. The mindless babbling from a sitcom on the television had replaced Christmas carols.

While there was no joy in the holidays after Ma, two years later there was the hope of joy. And Paris factored squarely into it. A New Year's Eve party would be the closest I'd come to having Christmas in my Paris place, for now.

To prepare for the party, I arrived a few days ahead, landing in Paris at seven in the morning. The sky was still black, with a full moon, when the taxi carried me to the apartment. The streets showed no signs of life, except for the twinkling swags of Christmas lights strung across. I was alone with my city, sharing a quiet moment before the fêtes began.

Leaning my jet-lagged head against the seat, I closed my eyes, feeling something I hadn't in a long time: peace.

In Paris, there were no connections to the past, only memories to be created.

As soon as I arrived at the apartment, I unpacked some battery-powered Christmas lights I'd brought to decorate for the party and strung them around the apartment—over the antique mirror, across the top of the shelves, in a glass bowl on the coffee table. With each strand I placed, instead of the tug of memory I felt in New York, I was filled with childlike excitement. It was as if, with this lighting ritual, I was casting out old ghosts and resetting the start date for my life.

New Year. New Me.

Jet lag still clung to me as I headed out, shopping list in hand, wheeling my caddy behind me. The gray sky threatened rain, but it was much milder than in New York, more like spring than winter. The streets were desolate except for one other shopper wheeling her own caddy filled with her own New Year's party goods. My shopping comrade. It still gave me a thrill to be able to join the locals in their everyday task of *en faisant les courses* even all these months later.

My long list included six bottles of champagne and party decorations, so I walked the extra five minutes to a Monoprix near Place de la Nation, where I knew I could find everything, even though I'd pay for the convenience.

When the sliding glass doors opened, I discovered where all my neighbors had been hiding. The whole of eastern Paris had the same idea.

Monoprix is to the French what Target is to Americans, although better, in my opinion, because it's filled with French things, including a huge selection of specialty foods. Even before I had the apartment, I'd shop at Monoprix for souvenirs and gifts. The Monoprix Nation is supposedly the biggest in Paris, and today it was packed with the whole of humanity shopping for their New Year's parties.

I was responsible for just a few specific items, so this should have been an easy get-in, get-out affair, but as soon as I entered the store, my plan was doomed. This was one of those evil genius corporate chains designed to put you off your game, with products curated and organized by color, texture, size, theme. They'd laid out all their best party fare right up front—pâtés, macaroons, chocolates, pastries, charcuterie—luring the unsuspecting and unfocused customer. Specialty vendors set up "pop-up" shops for the occasion, where we could sample wares from their purveyors: a pork and pistachio sausage from Lyon, called *cervelas*; Provençale aïoli, a garlicky mayonnaise; foie gras from the Périgord region. Drawn to one gleaming product display after another, and with an empty stomach, I wandered far off track, completely at the mercy of the merchandisers.

Six champagne showcases, towers of gleaming green glass with dazzling foil-stamped labels, advertised discounted prices. I stood gaping, incapacitated by indecision. The salesman was taking his time with a patron; I chewed over the price of the *blanc de blancs*: Was it a deal for twenty-one euros a bottle after the exchange rate? Were all the champagnes a good quality? This was France, right? Should I just grab six and go?

Ten minutes passed, and the salesman was still occupied. Anxiety setting in, I decided to come back to this section later.

Everything was bigger and better at this store. The cheese and meat counters were twenty feet long; there were five aisles just for dairy, with hundreds of products I'd never seen before, even after ten years of coming to Paris. Fig-flavored yogurt? Chocolate *fromage blanc*? Impossible to refuse.

Boudin (blood sausage), sliced brioche loaf, rose champagne cookies, truffle salt—it all ended up in my cart, whether it was on the list or not.

Which was fine, because I'd lost the list a while back.

Three hours later, I lumbered out of the store, dragging my bulging caddy and a huge overstuffed tote that I'd had to purchase just to carry everything I'd bought that was *not* on my list.

My heart pumped hard as I walked around Place de la Nation and toward home—maybe from the weight of my packages, or maybe from the extraordinary, sensual spree I'd just been on. Who knew shopping for a party could be a spiritual experience? Only in Paris.

I got all the way home before I realized I'd forgotten the champagne.

A wine merchant is called the *caviste*, and there is one just at the end of my street. Convenient, but my fear of French kept me away on most days. However, this was an emergency. Champagne was needed, and since my legs were still wobbly from hauling fifty pounds of groceries up two winding flights of stairs, the little wine shop around the corner was just the thing. I'd just have to get over myself and get the job done.

"Bonjour," I peeped, entering the shop, which still had its original nineteenth-century floor tiles, the stylized floral pattern worn away near the door from generations of wine-buying Parisians. Bottles of wine from every region in France lined the walls, their dimpled bottoms shining in the daylight streaming in from large leaded-glass windows. I wanted to try every one of these wines, just not all at once. At least not today. Today, it was about champagne.

The owner was nowhere in sight, so I *bonjour*'d again.

A tall, slender man in his mid-thirties with shaggy, dark blond hair appeared from the stock room. "Bonjooour," he sang.

Wowza. My face went warm. "Bonjour," I said again. "Je cherche quelques bouteilles de champagne pour une fête. Pas trop cher."

I hoped that I'd said I was looking for some bottles of inexpensive champagne, not a booty of champagne with too much Cher in it.

"I have these faw faw. Faw and fawfaw." His brown eyes shone. "You'd like?"

Yeah, sure, sweetie. Whatever you said. I'll take a case.

"Or I have these here," he continued. "They are lighter and very good. I drink this myself."

What was this? No *faw-faws*? Had I just understood every word? Maybe all this talk of wine was loosening my inhibitions.

"I like light," I parroted, examining the man's fine, pore-free skin, his high cheekbones and perfect slim nose.

He showed me an array of other champagnes, his long fingers teasing the products, and me.

It was a perfect time to try a phrase my friend Fabien had taught me, so I introduced myself and told my new *caviste*, "Je viens d'acheter un appartement dans le quartier." I explained that I'd just bought my apartment and pointed up the street to indicate just how close I was to him.

His eyes popped; he smiled wide. "So great! You come from where?" *Tu viens d'où?*

I realized he'd been using *tu* with me, the familiar version of "you." The French are very picky about how they address one another. Being too informal too soon could put you in a social pickle. Usually, a shop owner would address you with the formal *vous*, keeping a safe distance, but my *caviste* was getting close and personal right away. Should a girl read into that?

"Je suis de New York," I replied.

"I love New York!" he said in accented English, just as I was getting the hang of things in French.

Well, at least my boyfriend-to-be was bilingual.

"I maybe will go there in the summer for vacations," he continued in his version of English. "You coming here how many times?"

How many times? Was that Franglais? Did he mean how many

times to the store? Had he already sussed out my penchant for wine—or my interest in him? "How many times will I be coming to Paris?"

"No, I mean you came in Paris often? For vacations?"

"Yes, for many years." Did that make me sound old? "And I decided to buy an apartment here."

"Super!" he said.

The French say "super" a lot, even the coolest of guys, which is odd to an American. It's so very *Brady Bunch*. "Gee, Marcia, that's sure super!" The French pronounce it, "su-PEHR," with the accent on the second syllable.

"You come here to live for your working?" he asked, wrapping my purchases in tissue paper.

For my "working." How adorable was this guy? I had to break the sad news that I wasn't living in Paris full-time, that my "working" was in New York. But I assured him he'd see me every six weeks. After all, I wanted him to know he shouldn't be discouraged should he want to pursue something less business related.

"It's really great what you are doing!" His eyes locked hard on mine. "So cool."

Yes, it's so cool to have such a handsome wine seller right on my street who spoke English, sort of. Michel, *le caviste*. I ended up buying the six bottles of champagne, plus four bottles of wine.

You know, as a gesture of goodwill.

"Merci, à bientôt!" he said, handing over my bags.

Oh, you'll see me soon, don't worry about that, mon cheri. I planned to be back *très bientôt*.

The New Year definitely looked promising.

Only candlelight illuminated my apartment—that and twinkling Christmas lights, just like Ma used to light on New Year's Eve. And my table overflowed with platters of food as hers used to, only this was a collective effort, by friends. The French make food the centerpiece of every gathering. Eating isn't about nourishment; it's an experience to be shared and savored. Like life.

We stood around the table, steadily picking away at the feast we'd prepared, drinking champagne, laughing. It being a mild, rainy night, we'd opened the windows and could hear music and laughter from other parties on my street. Ours was a small group, but we held our own with the rest, filling my studio wall to wall with our energy. Anyone hearing us from the street would have thought there were twenty of us, the volume and intensity of the revelry outsize, as if we'd waited all year for this chance to let go. At least that's how I felt.

From time to time, I found myself just observing, enjoying my guests enjoying themselves: Geoffrey doubled over in laughter at something Christophe had said, Fabien's eyes wide with delight in reaction to a bite of food, Yann shimmying spontaneously to the music, Andrea chattering away in her Canadian-accented French.

Over the years, I'd catch my mother having a private moment like this, silently observing us during a boisterous Christmas dinner or New Year's Eve party, a hint of a smile on her face. I used to wonder what she was thinking, but now I understood. I felt it, too: this joy was of my making.

Ma was at her best when she was the hostess, cooking for a houseful. She was in her element, surrounded by the people she loved in a moment of bliss she'd created. There's a reason my happiest childhood memories were of my parents' parties, because Ma was at her happiest then. Bringing joy to others makes you someone, makes you worthy.

The cries of "Bonne Année!" echoing in the street signaled the New Year. We added our *youpis* to theirs.

Even though it was only six in the evening back home, I called my sister. Next year, I told her, I wanted to ring in the New Year with her in my Paris apartment. No arguments.

After the New Year came in, we moved the party to around the coffee table, where we ate and drank some more. It wasn't Ma's pizza, but it still hit home.

We went through five bottles of champagne and two bottles of wine—and that long list of food we'd put together turned out not to be so long; we'd eaten our way through most of it. Success. Ma would have been proud.

Paris was the only place I could have celebrated the coming year, in the apartment that brought me hope. Maybe this New Year, I could finally be optimistic about what was to come. I was ready to move past the pain.

New year. New life.

Eleven

When God Closes a Door, He Kicks You Out a Window

There's a restructure. They're breaking up the groups," my boss and friend of twenty years told me, closing my office door behind her and sitting down.

"What does *that* mean?" I asked. My chest tightened. I was a group director. Was I out of a job?

"We're figuring it out," she promised. "But I want you to know what's going to be happening today so you can tell your team." She listed some top people who would be leaving the company: our beloved editor in chief; the director of digital; the company's editorial director, one of the most respected veterans in the industry.

Out with the old, in with the scary unknown.

That was just the beginning. A change of CEO signaled sweeping changes across the company. The "Goodbye, and thank you for fifteen wonderful years" emails were becoming a staple in our inboxes, as were the groans of disappointment they'd create, which were relayed from office to office as each discovered the news. *Not another one.* I would go to more farewell cocktail parties in the months that followed than in my entire seven years at the company.

Would mine be next?

"Everything is changing," I cried on the phone to my sister as I walked home from the subway. "Everyone I love is leaving. The people who know my value to the company. And they're taking away all my directors."

"What do you mean?" my sister asked.

"There are no more groups, Ree! I'm not a group director anymore. They're all reporting to the marketing directors of their brands now."

In a way, this was my own fault. A lover of structure and efficiency, I'd reorganized my large art department into brand teams, each with a director reporting to me. Each director was responsible for day-to-day oversight of her brand, and each had her own design team.

In other words, I'd done a bang-up job of making myself redundant.

"I'm so screwed."

"Don't cry, Lee. You saved money, right?"

"Yes, I saved money!" I was well on my way to hysterical, racked by body-shaking sobs. It wasn't about the money. "But I don't want it to end!"

I loved this job—it was one of those life-altering, destiny-defining gigs that make you pinch yourself. I worked my whole career to get to this company, and every day when the elevator doors opened and I saw that world-famous logo on the wall, I'd think, *I can't believe I work here*. It never got old.

I had given up an opera singing career to take this job. Or at least my pursuit of the *dream* of having an opera singing career. I'd been performing in my spare time while my career in publishing continued on its own upward trajectory. But after the terror attacks of September 11, 2001, I'd decided, as many did, to seize the day and went for an opera career full bore. I took a part-time position as a creative director and focused fully on singing—taking two voice lessons a week, music and language coaching on weekends, and going on several auditions a month.

But five years later, I was broke, my vision of singing at the Met fading into the distance. Then my friend came to me with an offer to work with her on the biggest magazine brand in the country. "You're the only one I want for this," she said.

I hesitated. I liked the pace of my life, and I was still holding out hope that my big break was just an audition away. "I don't really want to work that hard anymore," I told my friend. I could only imagine the pressure and stress, the long hours. Did I really want to go back to that?

The job was top creative director over a huge team, including writers, Web and print designers, and a video editor. I'd have plenty of support and resources to get the job done, and with writers reporting to me, I could really shape the brand messaging in a way I never could before. The money was more than I'd ever been offered, more than double what I was currently making. It was terribly tempting. I wasn't a kid anymore; I had very little savings and an itsy IRA.

But I worried that this was another test by the universe to see how committed I was to my music. Other offers had come, and I'd always said no. No thank you. No, not now. No, not for me.

What would happen if, for once, I said yes?

After my first day on the job, though, I knew I'd made the best decision of my career. At the end of my first week, while reviewing a project with a colleague, I admitted, "I'm pretty sure I'm staying here until I die."

She nodded. "That's my plan."

Everyone I worked with seemed to be having the same love affair with the company. The passion was contagious. The pace, the energy, the senior level of talent—this was the big time. It stretched me in every direction, challenged what I thought I knew. The experience impacted my life outside the office, too. I was writing better, accomplishing more, taking more chances. Before this job, I wasn't fully committed to my design career, but, it turned out, I also wasn't fully committed to my opera career. When you're a creative person, you can't be halfway about any part of your life because it bleeds into everything. My new job kicked my life into high gear.

Seven years later, I had grown personally and professionally. The job didn't hurt my bank account, either. It allowed me to buy my apartment in Paris, and I couldn't be more grateful.

What would my life be like if it all went away? Here, at this company, I had purpose; I mattered. And what about my colleagues, my friends? I couldn't imagine not seeing them every day anymore. After seven years, they were family.

My sister told me not to worry. "It's going to be okay, Lee."

"I know," I said, even though I was pretty sure it would not be okay.

I was already mourning the end.

Christophe & Geoffrey Are Happy to Invite You to Their Wedding on the 17th May in the Town Hall of the 11th Arrondissement, Paris.

A black envelope addressed in a looping hand contained a card announcing the wedding of the year.

One of my friends at work called these events "LFTs," or "Look-Forward-Tos." Everyone needed them, she said: something fun in the future to plan for, especially when you're going through a rough patch. The first time she told me about the LFT, my mother was in the hospital. The LFT Ma and I talked about was Paris in April. She wouldn't make it to April, or to Paris, but the LFT served its purpose: it lifted her up when things felt hopeless.

The uncertainty of the situation at work had intensified, the usually boisterous atmosphere now laden with dread. People gathered in offices, whispering. The pressure to perform crippled us, squeezing the joy out of the job.

In the middle of it all, an invitation for the wedding of Geoffrey and Christophe came in the mail. My LFT had arrived.

Gay marriage had just become legal in France, and my friends were among the first to sign up for a license to make their six-year relationship legal in the eyes of the republic. This was more than a wedding; it was part of history.

Once the planning was under way, the wedding was pretty much all Geoffrey talked about. The theme: the 1920s. The color scheme: black, white, and gray. The playlist: epic. "Get ready to dance, my Liza!"

The invitation remained tacked to the bulletin board above my computer monitor, where I could see it all day. Paris was yet again the bright spot in a dark time.

The mairie, or "town hall," of the 11th arrondissement sits on Place Léon Blum in the center of my district. Each of the twenty districts of Paris has a town hall, often a grand château dating from the eighteenth or nineteenth century. In Paris, one goes to his respective town hall instead of the city hall, Hôtel de Ville, for most municipal functions, including marriages.

This wasn't just any wedding; this wedding had a themed dress code. It was a production. You couldn't throw on any old cocktail dress—no, no. This required real planning. I'd started shopping as soon as I received the invitation.

One of our gang, Yann, was my date for the wedding. A dandy with a penchant for English tailors, Yann set the bar high for us. He and I started talking about our outfits a month before. Should we coordinate? How much did we want to embrace the 1920s theme? Emails of ideas were sent back and forth; I'd show him outfits via video chat so he could give me a thumbs-up or -down. It was the perfect diversion from the drama at work, and I threw myself into it.

When the day arrived, it turned out neither of us had stuck to the 1920s theme, but we did honor the color scheme. Well, sort of—with him in gray tweed with slim-fitting pants and tan brogues, and me in a huge black, ankle-length ruffled skirt cinched at the waist and a bold black-and-white horizontal-striped crop top. I looked more like a flamenco dancer than a flapper, but we made a smashing couple as we walked toward the mairie under a cerulean sky, causing a stir as we passed the humble cafés on Boulevard Voltaire. Perhaps we were a bit de trop—too much—for the neighborhood, but this was the wedding of the year after all.

The guests mingled on the square outside the town hall, all black, white, and gray—straw hats, sequined headbands, knee pants, spectator shoes—a frame from an old silent film superimposed on the modern world.

When the grooms arrived, we entered the building, our voices echoing in the cavernous reception hall as we climbed the marble stairs to the salon where the wedding was to be held. More like a chamber in Versailles than a room in a municipal building, the space was paneled in mahogany with a thirty-foot trompe l'oeil ceiling. The guests craned their heads upward as they took their seats, marveling at the majestic surroundings.

The ceremony was only fifteen minutes long from the "Welcome friends and family" speech to the signing of the wedding registry. The tissue clutched in my hand didn't even have a chance to see action.

But this would not be a day for tears.

After the ceremony, we walked en masse from the town hall to Geoffrey and Christophe's apartment for a goûter, small bites served with nonalcoholic punch. Geoffrey had upped the ante for his own standard of epic for this party. They'd transformed their entire home into a 1920s artist's studio, complete with the requisite photo call wall where we posed with props from les années '20s. Images of silent film stars, and Geoffrey's own 1920s-inspired drawings, hung on the walls. The usual contents of the bookshelves had been swapped out for antiquated curios, and vintage books and magazines. They'd even brought in an old Victrola for the music. Anyone looking in from across the courtyard would have thought we'd gotten stuck in time, a party on a loop for decades.

The guests were packed into the small apartment, spilling out into the hall, their voices and energy overflowing the space. I was in the room with them, but not really present. Behind my smile, worry about the future of my job wormed around in my head, making me feel brittle. The heavy dose of euphoria in the room was overwhelming, its abundance in hard contrast to the daily commiseration I'd been immersed in at work. Instead of taking part, I went around collecting empty cups and discarded plates, refilling the platters of cookies, getting drinks for the rest of the guests. I couldn't let go. I didn't know how.

For now, it was just enough to let the party swirl around me. All I could manage were small sips of their exuberant air.

The reception, or le dîner, was being hosted at a friend's apartment in the 9th arrondissement, so the entire party, fifty of us, rode the Métro together, filling an entire car. Our fellow riders eyed us, whispered to one another. Crammed in with the rest in the train car, all of us unified by our monochromatic garb, I found it harder to deny that I was part of the celebration.

"Excuse me, mesdames et messieurs," the maid of honor announced to the riders, whose space we'd invaded, "Please join us in congratulating the grooms, Geoffrey and Christophe, on their marriage!"

Applause erupted in the train car.

Goose bumps popped up on my arms. Far from the overblown ballroom affairs I was used to, this was intimate and real—shared by the community.

As we arrived at our stop, instead of the automated announcement, we heard the conductor's voice: "This station is Bonne Nouvelle. Let's salute the happy couple as they exit the train." He even honked the horn as the train pulled away.

We stood on the platform laughing, waving like royalty to the passengers, who waved in return, their smiling faces filling the windows of the cars. This was unimaginable in New York. The only time a New York subway conductor interrupts the automated message is to scream at someone for holding the doors.

We paraded through the district, toward the apartment where the reception was being hosted. With each shop or café we passed, people would come out onto the sidewalk and applaud, shouting "Felicitations!" to our wedding party.

I wasn't content anymore with sips of joyful air. Now I sucked it in and let it fill me up. Who cared what was happening back at work? I wasn't going to miss any more of this day wrapped up in worry.

The reception was intimate, too, a simple catered house party put together by Geoffrey, in a lovely top-floor apartment with a terrace overlooking the rooftops of the neighborhood. The sun shone on us as we began the party, and by the time it sank below the skyline, we were in full club mode, a frenzy of stomping feet and waving arms, until we collapsed, sweaty and exhausted, on the terrace under the stars.

"My Liza!" Geoffrey said, flopping into a chair beside mine. "Are you happy?"

"So happy," I told him. So, *so* happy.

I wanted to hold this day in my hands and carry it back to New York, where I needed some joy.

Or maybe I should just stay here where I was happier?

The first round of layoffs passed me over, and I was feeling more confident that they meant to hang on to me, but the company didn't resemble itself anymore. Most of the department heads, from consumer marketing to the business office, were gone. Our resources had been slashed; we were working harder with fewer people.

We weren't alone. The entire magazine publishing world felt as if it were imploding, and I was no longer sure I wanted to stay in it until I died.

At the wedding in Paris, I had glimpsed a happier life that made me dare to imagine more for myself. I could create a new career as a writer, maybe, or become a marketing consultant—something that might allow me to spend more time in my other city.

But could I walk away from everything I knew, even when it wasn't making me happy anymore? If I could, it would be the first time in my life.

A friend had recommended a life coach a few months before, someone who could help unstick me from my fears, but I hadn't contacted her. I'd been telling myself I'd figure it out, or that something would fall into place. But nothing had, and things were actually getting worse. Backed into a corner by my own fear and helplessness, I finally reached out and started working with the life coach every week.

My role at work had been diminished from overseeing a group of six magazines to heading creative for only one. They compensated by enlarging my title from creative director to executive director, creative. I was trying to make the most of things, as I always do, making a banquet out of crumbs, telling myself I should be grateful just to have a seat at the table. After all, they had given me the largest, most prestigious brand to work on—and that was something, right? And it wasn't terrible; it was freeing to be able to focus on one brand. I had an endless stream of ideas, and the energy and focus to realize them. Maybe I could stick it out until that big chunk of stocks became vested the following February—or longer, if things improved.

Just as I was settling into the rhythm of my new role, the last crumbs I'd been subsisting on were swept away.

"I have to cut two from your team," my new VP of marketing told me, gray-faced.

I plunked down heavily in the chair across from hers. My New York life was becoming smaller and smaller, harder and harder. We were already pared down so lean from the last two layoffs, and this being the largest magazine, it meant the most work: a relentless stream of creative requests. We were starting to fall behind. "We can't do this job with only three people. I used to have fifteen."

"I know," she said, still pale. "I told them that." But it didn't matter.

I assessed what would be left of my team: my digital director, my design director, my copy director, and me. That was a lot of directors. Who would do the little day-to-day jobs: the promotional emails, the client invitations? Was I expected to do that as well as the huge, strategic projects they needed me for? Was I just being a prima donna? An ingrate?

My quality of life evaporated in front of me, along with my plumb job. I'd be churning out mind-numbing doodads all day long, on an endless assembly line. Call me a prima donna, but my career had just regressed fifteen years.

And what about Paris? My steady diet of Paris visits was the thing that kept me going, but with my support team cut, I'd be lucky if I could get away twice a year, as I used to before buying the apartment.

I could swallow almost anything, but going backward? No.

I found myself asking the same question I'd asked when my mother died: Now what?

"ASK FOR A PACKAGE!"

My life coach offered this solution, screaming at me in all caps, when I emailed her about the latest developments at work. We'd had a coaching session that morning, a great one where I uncovered the emotional drivers that had gotten me through life, but that were now holding me back: fear and guilt. Then I defined my new drivers: self-nurturing and thriving. It was an ecstatic start to a day that went south fast.

My coach's advice stunned me. I wasn't ready to do something like that. Could I give up a steady paycheck? A big fat one, at that?

Yes, the layoffs were a horrible turn of events, but ask for a package? Dreaming of change was one thing, but actually forcing the hand of fate? Madness.

A decision this big called for crowd-sourcing, polling the masses. It's always the way I make life-changing choices, talking to at least a dozen people before I decide which way to go. Exhausting, yes, but it's what I need, and I needed it for this. On the call list: my sister; my childhood friend-cum-brother, Steven; a former boss; and an ex-colleague. Mostly they listened, but no one could really tell me what to do.

That was something my mother was good at.

One of my closest friends, Matthew, whom I'd met many years before at *Mademoiselle* magazine, was a design entrepreneur with his own fashion label. Matthew was so smart, and he knew me better than anyone. Matthew would have the answers.

He invited me to his studio, where I found another of our designer friends, Lapo, working on a project for Matthew. This was a boon, since no one is freer with opinions than my Florentine friend Lapo—and I could count on him to give me the most practical advice.

They listened as I spelled out my situation, as I'd already done six times: how we'd have to do the work of ten with a skeleton crew, but that I'd been assured freelance support, so maybe the work could still get done. As I was talking, something occurred to me that hadn't before: "I'm already so tired."

As soon as I admitted it, I crumbled. I *was* tired. For over a year we'd lived with the boom hanging over our heads—reorganizations, layoffs, rumors of being sold, stress for the sake of stress. "I'm just so, so tired."

"Ask for a package," Matthew said, tossing it off as if he were saying, "Have a cookie."

There it was again, that crazy advice. That's not what I wanted to hear. Who did they think I was? A big, bold move like that? And then what? "I'd be walking away from a really good paycheck."

And health insurance, and bonuses, and stock options. "I'm not ready."

"Lisa, you're fine! You *have* money. Go to Paris. Write! You were just profiled in *New York* magazine! What more do you need?"

That "money" he was referring to was my retirement fund. I'd spent seven years building that safety net for my old age. I didn't want to piss it away. That wasn't responsible. "I'm a saver, not a spender."

Matthew shook his head. "You have that money so you can build your new career. This is what you've been waiting for." Then he told me I should probably see a therapist about my money fears. "Why do you think you're going to be poor?"

Because I'd struggled before, in my twenties, and it was terrifying. Borrowing money for rent, living on credit cards. It was years ago, but an experience like that sticks with you. One year, I made only seven thousand dollars. That was the lowest point.

For fifteen years I didn't have to worry about money. It just appeared in my bank account, freeing me to focus on other things. Did I want to give up that kind of security?

"I think it's an easy decision," Lapo finally chimed in.

Oh, good, I thought. My practical friend would be the voice of reason.

"You could die tomorrow," he said. "What good is the money then? Be happy. Now."

You could die tomorrow. Lapo chose this analogy because his own mother was dying of cancer, and he was discovering for himself the fragility and vulnerability of life, just as I had done when Ma died.

"Why do you want to stay in your job?" Lapo asked. "What are the reasons?"

I calculated my expenses: my mortgage; the two expensive storage facilities filled with my mother's and aunt's things; maintenance and utility bills in two cities. Taxes. I saw the faces of my team, my friends at work, when they'd learn I was bailing on them. I thought of Ma, who'd been so proud I had this job that she used to carry around my business cards to show her friends.

My reasons for staying were all about fear and guilt, those old motivators that were holding me back.

My New York life had hit a wall, while life in Paris was expanding all the time. Paris had given me the purpose I was missing after my mother died. All the signs were pointing in one direction.

Maybe you deserve more.

I'd spent all this time laying the groundwork for the next phase in my life, whether I'd realized it or not. Matthew was right: I should go to Paris and write. I had the means; I had the opportunity. Sure, nothing was certain, but if not now, when?

Seven years almost to the day after I called my friend to tell her I would take the incredible job she'd offered, I called to ask, "What if I were the one to be laid off?"

I took the package.

PART 3

Fear and Self-Loathing in Paris

· Twelve ·

Living the Dream?

Three suitcases, two laptops, one carry-on—that's what you need when you're about to "live the dream" in Paris for two months.

I'd sent my own "Goodbye and thank you" email to my colleagues, toasted them at my farewell cocktail party. After one last look at my view of the Hudson River from my twenty-eighth-floor corporate office, I walked away.

Stacked in a corner of my New York apartment, boxes filled with files and projects from nearly every magazine I'd ever worked at—my entire career's portfolio, one box for every year in the business. These things had moved with me from one job to the next, but this time, even though I'd packed and labeled each box with care, I wondered if I'd ever open them again.

Was I really moving on for good?

During those first few days, I drifted around my apartment. I'd dust something in one corner of the room then stop midway and sweep up in another; start packing for Paris but end up cleaning out a kitchen drawer. One day, thirty minutes was spent lining up all the spines of my books on my living room shelves so they were flush.

Unemployed.

Without someone else's demands defining my day, I didn't know what to do. As the weeks wore on, the languid pace of my new life disoriented me. I invented errands, scheduled lunches, anything to fill a calendar that was suddenly blank. I was used to six meetings a day, multiple deadlines, one hundred fifty emails in my inbox. Now life had stopped dead.

Unemployed.

I should have been elated. I was free to live the life I'd dreamed for myself.

Years before, in a writers' workshop, I'd had to create a bio for my imaginary dust jacket as a visualization exercise. Even then I knew what I wanted the first line of my future to look like: "Anselmo, who splits her time between New York and Paris . . ." It felt improbable, but I wrote it anyway. Now it was placed right in my hands.

Future me was present me.

But I was still stuck in past me. As the date for my departure arrived, a wave of New York nostalgia washed over me. Like those first few days after you break up with someone, New York was suddenly the most amazing, most beautiful city in the world. Summer was just getting started; the weather was extraordinary every day. The outdoor cafés were filling with people, the parks coming to life. This was my favorite time of year in New York.

"I don't want to leave," I told my doorman, Carl, teary-eyed as I waited for my car to the airport. "What's wrong with me?"

I finally had what I wanted, and now I didn't want it?

Not ready to move on, I was still hanging on to something. That's probably why I was hauling three suitcases of stuff from my New York life to Paris.

I'd untethered myself from my former life, and now I was flailing around, loosey-goosey, without a plan or roadmap.

But I got myself on that plane, white knuckles and all, because forward was the only choice I'd given myself.

It was Paris or bust.

The taxi entered Paris city limits at Porte de Vincennes, near my district. As soon as I caught sight of the Castorama, and the eighteenth-century columns flanking Place de la Nation, my heartbeat sped up. I was home.

New York was a memory.

As we turned onto my street, I could see my *caviste*, Michel, in his shop. I waved, even though I knew he couldn't see me. It was for me, anyhow, saying hello to my Paris life, restarting what had been on pause until now.

Eight full weeks stretched out before me. Who knows what might happen with my favorite wine seller? After a few weeks of seeing each other, me in my cute summer outfits, maybe things could move from my buying wine to our drinking it together on a picnic blanket on the Seine—forever.

Eight weeks. I would develop a routine, build on my relationships, *really* live in my neighborhood. Finally. All I had to do was get my three suitcases, two laptops, and one carry-on up two flights of stairs.

"Do you need help with those?" a voice asked in French.

A man in paint-spattered clothes appeared on the landing, one flight up. Behind him, a cloud of plaster dust, and the *thump! thump!* of hammers coming from one of the apartments. A new neighbor?

"Oui, merci!" I said. "Merci beaucoup." He had to be an angel, and I told him so.

He waved a hand in front of his face, deflecting the compliment, mouthed *pas de tout*: "not at all."

"Were you away a long time?" he asked, huffing as he carried both my largest suitcases to my floor.

I explained in my own version of French that I was from New York and would be staying awhile. "Lots of clothes."

"You're from America?" His eyes brightened. "I have a cousin there!" He named a place that sounded like *Caroleen d'Sood*. It took a second to register that he was actually talking about a state in my own country, South Carolina, the last place I'd have expected a Parisian to choose.

"He works there?" I asked.

"No, he likes the beaches."

Really, more than those in the South of France? I'd been to the beaches in South Carolina, and they're swell, but still. To me, after going through so much to live in France, I couldn't imagine anyone wanting to abandon this paradise for Myrtle Beach. But I suppose the grass is always *plus vert* on the *autre côté* of the fence.

Now here was a man with family in down-home U.S.A. appearing just when I needed help with my luggage. Everything was already going my way in Paris.

The satisfying click of my unlocking door sent a rush through me. I took a deep breath and pushed the door open. *I'm home.*

In the next instant I was coughing. A wall of mustiness hit me in the face: the acrid smell of mold and something else. Was that *sewage*?

My body tried to cough up the spores I'd just inhaled. When that didn't work, the opening of my windpipe narrowed down to a pinhole.

What the hell?

The leak was not a surprise. A few months back, I'd discovered some minor bubbling near the baseboard in my entryway. My contractor, Aiden, addressed it with the building's managing agent, *le syndic*, whose plumber opened a hole in my bathroom to uncover the source. They finally found it, they'd said, in the shower of the apartment above mine. Simple. Done and done.

Fabien, who'd stopped by my place to drop off my mail, warned me that the bubbling had gotten a little worse since I'd seen it months before. "There is a smell of humidity," he wrote in an email to me. "It's not very nice."

Not very *nice*? It smelled like a swamp had seeped in through my plumbing. I threw the windows wide open and grabbed the fan from my closet, cranking it up all the way to suck in fresh air.

Normally, I'd have unpacked my bags and settled in, but no way could I stay in this stink. I sprinted to the store and stocked up on candles, incense, disinfectant sprays—anything that had a pleasant scent.

Between the sweet-smelling candles and the air now circulating in the apartment, it seemed pretty certain that, in an hour or so, things would improve. The problem was probably just a residual odor from moisture that had been sealed in my empty apartment for the last two months. And I wasn't too worried about the additional bubbling, because my contractor had told me that might happen, even after the leak was repaired, as the water settled out. "We'll fix that right up," he had said.

I unpacked my three suitcases, set up my laptops, and emptied my carry-on. Let the living begin!

While hanging up the last of my clothes, a pretty North African woman wearing a colorful head scarf appeared at my door, which was opened to draw more air from the windows. She introduced herself as the renter who lived above me. Then she and her ebullient energy pushed their way inside my apartment to have a look at the damage the leak had caused.

"Oh, it's nothing!" she said with a huge smile. *Mais, c'est rien!*

Nothing? Could she not see the wall of bubbles? I demonstrated how the sliding door to the bathroom no longer glided.

"Me, I can't use my shower," she said. "It's horrible. They put plastic up where the leak is and I have to shower with a cup!"

Wait a minute—*what?* Had I understood her correctly? "The leak isn't repaired?" *Pas réparée?*

"No, no," she sang, still smiling. "You own the apartment?"

I nodded, dazed. How was the leak not repaired yet?

"You're the owner? Unbelievable! But you are so young!"

She walked into the main living space and had a look around. "It's very nice! You took the wall away. I like it!"

I thanked her, assuring her I wasn't so young as I gently cor-
ralled her back to the bubbling wall—and the issue at hand. For
once, I wasn't interested in exchanging pleasantries with a neighbor, and my mind was spinning too fast to hear anything but *fawfaw*
anyway.

I asked her in my simple French why the leak had not been repaired after all this time. It had been five months since I notified
the managing agent of the first signs of bubbling.

She shrugged, still smiling. "But this is normal in France!"

It's normal to let a leak destroy someone's property? That's not
how it worked in New York. Leaks happened, the managing agent
responsible for protecting the owner's investment sent a plumber
the next day, and the problem was fixed. It wasn't complicated.

This leak was creating havoc for us both, so why wasn't my
neighbor as angry as I was?

"Anyway, it was nice to meet you," she said, moving toward the
door. "You come for couscous one night soon, yes?"

"Sure. Thank you." If this had been six months ago, I'd have
set a date, but all I could think about was getting her out the door
and firing off an email to the managing agent.

These people have no idea who they're dealing with, I told myself. Now that
I was in town, I would get things moving. Maybe the French move
slowly, but they hadn't met me. I'd worked at a weekly magazine. I
knew how to get things done. Chop, chop, people!

I was about to get my first lesson in how things work in France.

The agent replied to my email and very politely, with all sympathy, told me that they'd like to help, but the location of the leak
put the responsibility in the hands of the owner with the leaky
shower stall. I should feel free to contact her and inquire.

So I did. The owner said, "Nope, not me," and kicked that hot
potato back to the managing agent.

Wasn't it just a simple repair? What could it cost? Five hundred
euros, tops?

This had to be a misunderstanding. I was sure there was something I could do. I called my very own property expert, Sarah, who had brokered the sale of the apartment and now helped manage its affairs. As it turned out, her agency was geared toward foreign property owners—just another one of those perks I'd sworn my mother had worked out for me from the beyond. Sarah's agency had set up my utilities, found my contractor and architect, and arranged my homeowner's insurance, which it looked like I was going to need now.

"I hate to tell you this," she said after hearing my tale, "but this is the worst possible scenario."

Worst possible scenario?

"Sorry," she said, "but you need to call a lawyer. It's the only way to prevent this from dragging on for years."

For *years*?

Fire had always been my biggest fear. Who'd have thought a flood would be the thing that would destroy my home?

Sarah explained that the lawyer would arrange for a court expert to settle the dispute so the repairs could proceed. Without the courts intervening, no one would repair the leak, because as soon as they did repair it, they'd be tacitly admitting responsibility for the damage done to my apartment.

Why had I bought a property in Paris? I didn't speak the language; how could I even call my insurance company? These people were going to walk all over me.

My hand became a fist around the phone. *Call a lawyer. Worst possible scenario.* This couldn't be happening. Not now, not to me. These horrible French people were flushing me out of my precious hideyhole. As if I didn't belong here.

Sarah gave me the name and number of her lawyer and told me to call him immediately. Time was of the essence, because the August vacations were upon us and everyone would disappear for at least three weeks or more. "Get it going now, and hopefully by September, you'll have a solution."

I'd come to Paris to sit in cafés and write my book. So much for that. Well, I'd wanted the real Paris experience. I just didn't think I'd get a lifetime's worth my first week.

"Quel putain de bordel de merde."

These words articulated the state of my apartment. They were also the first words out of Christophe's mouth when he visited with Geoffrey and Fabien and saw my bubbling wall for the first time.

Quel putain de bordel de merde is one of those untranslatable French expressions that, once you get the hang of it, you really grow to appreciate—the perfect proportion of vulgarity, emotion, and poetry that only the French can achieve.

Putain, or "whore," is a word I've heard tossed off a lot, the way we'd say, "Crap," or its crasser variation. *Whore, I'm cold! My whore of a car won't go. Oh, whore, that was funny!*

Bordel is "whorehouse." But *quel bordel!* is what you hear in place of the English "What a mess!"—but only for the worst of messes. I figure the reason is because what happens to you in a whorehouse is precisely how you feel when the universe does a number on you. Oh so French, *mais non*?

Christophe was dead right: the state of my apartment *was* a whore of a whorehouse of shit.

"Oh, my Liza!" Geoffrey chimed in. "What are you going to do? When we had the leak in our kitchen, it took a year."

A *year*? So Sarah was right.

Fabien took a whiff as he walked into the apartment. "Oh, sweetie! But the smell is much, much better!" He rubbed my back as if he were afraid Christophe's assessment might have upset me. "Really, it is."

Fabien had elected himself caretaker of my place, checking on it every week, taking in the mail. When he started cleaning and doing my laundry, I made him my official property manager. Why shouldn't everyone benefit? We'd met through Geoffrey, bonding over shoes: screaming-neon-orange sneakers. I knew him all of thirty minutes at the time. He was walking me to the Métro when he suddenly stopped at a store window, reeled back, threw up his hands, and let loose a high-pitched "Eeeeeee!" It was love—for him with the shoes, for me with him. He wore those orange sneakers all the time now. Tonight was no exception.

"Did you find everything was nice when you arrive?" he asked me.

"Yes, sweetie, everything was perfect. Except for the smell."

"It's such a big sheet!" Fabien did not mean bed linens; he meant *bordel de merde*. And yes, it was, but having my friends in my apartment helped me feel less vulnerable and hopeless. Their energy filled the place, buoying me.

The usual overabundance of cocktail foods had been laid out. My favorite cheeses: a firm Cantal, a creamy St. Félicien. Of course, there had to be a charcuterie platter, of cured *jambon* (ham), dried sausages, and pâté. Lots of wine and bread. It was always tricky when it came to serving Fabien. Not only was he a vegetarian, but he was allergic to chocolate and cheese. On top of that, he didn't drink wine. How he survived in France, I don't know. For him, I usually made crudités and my "famous" endive and pear salad— so called because I made it all the time.

Each time I entertained, I tended to serve the same thing, with a few variations, and I did worry a bit that my friends might be growing tired of my lack of imagination. Did they text one another about it?

Cocktail party at Liza's tonight. You going?

Yeah. Get ready for endive salad again.

Does she know we have hundreds of cheeses here? Always Cantal.

Maybe I was just being insecure. My friends seemed completely content at my parties, devouring everything I served, every time. And when they entertained, they served simple meals, too. No one made elaborate dinners; few had real ovens, mostly counter-top microwave/grill combos. It was often salads and dips, something sweet for dessert from the local *patisserie*, such as *tarte tatin*, an upside-down apple cake, served with *crème fraîche*. There were some staples at everyone's *cocktail dinatoire* beyond bread and cheese that I wouldn't have expected. Fake crab sticks were wildly popular, and fruit juices, grapefruit or strawberry being the top favorites. I always made sure I had those on hand, but drinking fruit juice while eating cheese? Not my thing, I didn't care how French it was.

It wasn't just about the food anyway; it was about sharing that food with others. The meal was the excuse to gather, and whatever you served, your guests were grateful for a seat at the table because you'd made them a part of your life.

I called it the French trinity: family, friends, and food. The simple pleasures were exalted in Paris and that always had a curative effect when I'd come for a visit. I'd thought it was because I was on vacation, far from my everyday troubles, yet now I was in the middle of big trouble with the leak, and it was even more true. Having my friends around my table made things feel normal again.

Seeing how complicated it was just to get a leak fixed had given me a taste of how hard life could be in Paris. None of my friends had it easy; they always seemed to be scraping to make ends meet, frustrated in dead-end jobs because they'd been pigeonholed in a system that allowed little room for career change after twenty. Regardless of their hardships, economic or otherwise, when we were together, their capacity for joy was boundless. And infectious.

We sat around the table, slathering cheese and fig jam on crusty baguettes, filling our glasses. The conversation wasn't deep—a concert at the Rex, the latest drama at Fabien's job, Geoffrey's new exhibition—but I was glad for the levity. After all, it was my welcome home party.

Eating, and watching my friends polish off the platters of food, had restored for me the purpose of my apartment, its role in my life as a giver of joy.

"It's too bad," Geoffrey said in French, "about that whore of a leak. Because this apartment is really special."

I woke up with my sinuses so impacted my teeth hurt. My eyes burned; my ears itched.

Oh no. *Mold.*

Of all the allergies I'd outgrown since childhood, mold was not one of them. One microscopic spore throws my body into histamine hyperdrive: the annoying cough, the watery eyes, the sneezing. Usually, I avoid moldy spaces, but this was my *home.*

My perfect Paris nest had a full-blown mold infestation.

I walked into the bathroom to find something to take for my headache. My reflection startled me: red eyes so swollen and misshapen that one was smaller than the other. I stared, fascinated and horrified at the same time. Was this real? Were the mold spores making me hallucinate?

I twisted the cold water tap, whipped a hand towel off the rack, and soaked it in cold water. I pressed the wet towel against my eyes, but it was going to take a lot more than that to fix my problems.

All the scented candles in the world couldn't mask the truth of what was happening. The lower half of the wall in my entryway was damp and distorted; the parquet flooring by the door was spongy. All of it creating the perfect Petri dish for mold to flourish.

That it was hidden from my sight only made the mold more sinister. I imagined a thick, hairy blanket of spore-spewing organisms creeping along the underside of my spongy parquet, crawling inside my damp walls, spreading all around me as I stood there wheezing.

It wasn't just a matter of cosmetic repairs to a bubbling wall anymore. The apartment would have to be dried out, and the mold remediated. I knew what was coming: They'd arrive with their sledgehammers and punch holes in my walls, crowbar my floor up, taking my blue kitchen unit with it—and leaving me with a pile of rubble all over again. I'd just built this home, and now it was going to have to be torn down.

That was only *after* the leak was fixed. How long would that take? How much more damage? My dream apartment was falling apart, and I couldn't fix it.

I tried to suck in air, but my chest tightened. My hands started to tingle. I felt nauseated, weak. Was I having a heart attack?

No, I knew what it was. This wasn't the first time.

I thought back to when Ma had been in the hospital a few weeks—more specifically, the hospital, then rehab, then the hospital again. She'd had kidney surgery, hip surgery. Now she was in the cardiology wing because she'd experienced heart failure.

Standing in the hallway outside Ma's room with my sister and our childhood friend Steven, I started to feel odd—nothing specific, just *off*, as if I were suddenly hollow and cool air were rushing through me. My chest began to tighten; a sharp, throbbing pain grabbed me just above my heart, wrapped around my side. A tingling rushed down my arms. I couldn't breathe.

"What is it?" Maria's eyes were wide with fear. "You're pale."

"I don't know." I described my symptoms. "I feel weird."

"Do you think it's your heart?" Steven asked. He stopped one of the nurses in the hall, but she told him they'd have to take me to Emergency in spite of the fact we were in the cardiology wing.

"I'll be okay," I said, trying to convince myself. There was no way I was going to die of a heart attack with Ma in the hospital. That was a disproportionate amount of tragedy for one family.

"You're scaring me," Maria said. "You're under too much stress. This is *too much stress!*"

She and Steven led me into the darkened antechamber outside Ma's room, sat me in a chair. They stood over me with terrified faces.

The floor was falling out from under me. I reached out with both hands, hooked my fingers around the belt loops of my sister's jeans, and pulled her close. Efforts to take in breath were fruitless; my chest grabbed tight.

I threw my head back and tried again to draw in breath. As I exhaled, my whole body shook. My sister shook with the force of it.

I was coming apart. I was dying right there in that frigging hospital.

"What's happening to me?" I said, panic-stricken.

It wasn't until I took another breath and exhaled that I realized I was sobbing.

The harder I sobbed, the better I felt. The tingling stopped, the chest pain eased.

I'd been holding it in for days, weeks, holding it together for Ma. My body was expressing itself even if I would not—through pain.

That was when I learned about somatization: emotion creating physical symptoms. And also when I learned about the wonders of antianxiety meds.

It would have been great to have some of those magic pills now, standing in the middle of the leaky mess that was my Paris home.

I took the compress off my eyes and stared in the mirror at my bloated face. All around me water had splashed—the sink, the floor tiles. I had done that when I made the compress, careless girl.

Helpless girl.

Stooping down, I mopped up the water with the towel I'd used for the compress.

Hard water spots on the faucet resisted me, no matter how vigorously I rubbed them. I took a sponge from under the sink and scrubbed until they were obliterated and my sink sparkled like the day we took it out of the box.

Good. Better.

But what was this dust on the shelving? Disgusting! I sponged that off, too.

Streaks on the tile suddenly popped out at me. Moisture that had dripped down after my daily showers, no doubt. They marred my clean white wall. I got the stepstool and buffed them off, wiped down every tile, all the walls. The ceiling.

While I was up there, I cleared the dust off the wall sconce and from the top of the cabinet. How could I not have seen that until now?

Better. Cleaner. Almost.

A few of my long hairs lay on the white bathroom floor, so I grabbed the mop from the closet and eliminated them. As long as I was mopping, why not attack the floor in the hallway, and the kitchen, and the living room?

I wiped down all the baseboards, eradicated every dust bunny.

Scrubbed a stain out of the area rug.

Vacuumed the curtains.

The last thing I did was move the kitchen table equidistant between the kitchen unit and the window. Then, placing a vase dead center, squared it precisely to the tabletop.

Now everything was perfect.

Except it wasn't.

9:30 A.M.; the 16th arrondissement.

The stark 1930s Modernist façade of the Palais de Chaillot dominated the plaza, and me, as I exited the Métro at Trocadéro. This district, ultrarich and rather stiff, had always intimidated me—or maybe it was just the impossibly thin women sashaying about in their minimalist shift dresses, Birkin bags swinging on their arms.

Unless I was visiting my banker, or one of the nearby museums, I rarely came here. It was mostly residential anyway: just rows and rows of pristine white-faced apartment buildings and very few local shops. When you have help to do your shopping for you, who needs a corner market?

Like Manhattan's Upper East Side, le Seizième was not for me.

Turning off Place du Trocadéro onto a wide boulevard, I glanced at an address I'd jotted down on a scrap of paper. By the time I looked up again, I had arrived at the building. An imposing, two-story, wrought-iron door made sure all who passed through understood the importance of the building's occupants.

You are going to see a lawyer—in Paris, I thought, unable to decide if this was a nightmare or an adventure.

The massive door did not give way easily, making me earn my access to the lobby. Inside, all was in marble—walls of white marble, floors in black. A grand staircase was also marble, its plush red carpeting shushing my footfall as I climbed, lest I disturb the important legal business happening behind the ten-foot-high wood-paneled doors, each with its own highly polished bronze plaque announcing, AVOCAT À LA COUR—"Lawyer of the Court."

Should a client feel as if she were in hostile territory?

The last time I was in a lawyer's office, my sister and I were visiting our mother's estate attorney. Maybe that was why I felt queasy now.

My lawyer's secretary greeted me politely and asked me to have a seat. I wiped my palms on my skirt. Since when did I have sweaty palms?

A young man in his early thirties came out and told me he was my lawyer. No stuffy navy suit, no intimidation. He was breezy and deliciously informal.

And really quite cute. He'd just tipped the scale from nightmare to adventure.

Sitting across from my cute, young lawyer—who, I hoped, had enough experience—I took out my laptop. With the situation in my apartment keeping me from writing, it looked like legal note-taking was the only action it was going to see for a while.

Apparently, according to him, my leak case wasn't unique. He had three others in the hopper just like it. One of his clients had a leak that had been carrying on for five years. *Five.* I was lucky, he told me, that mine was only a few months old. But I'd still need patience.

"Zuh process," he told me in thickly accented English, "eez slow but fair."

"How slow?"

He explained that it being the end of July was already a challenge, but if he got the case in front of a judge before the August holidays, when the courts went into recess, we could get lucky. "An expert could be assigned to your case as early as October."

October was *early?*

That would be ideal, because the expert could take two to three more months before he was free to examine my situation. Once he did, *hopefully* he'd make his recommendation a few weeks after that. Or a month. Or so.

I added it up in my head. Where did that put me? March? This was July. How much more leak damage might I suffer by then?

"Then there is the deliberation period," he continued.

The *what?*

The parties concerned are permitted to debate the expert's decision. "If that happens, you must go to the judge to decide." But I'd pay for that in more euros and more time. "Hopefully, that won't happen."

The process is slow . . .

"You are zuh victim 'ere, madame," he said. "Do not worry. You will be recompensed for your prejudice."

I strained to understand him through his accented English— and the blood whirring in my ears. Recompense my prejudice? Was that legalese, or was he speaking Geoffrey-isms, Anglicizing French legal terms? "My expenses will be paid?"

"By zuh responsible party, yes. The judge will award you for your prejudice." I didn't have to prove anything; it wasn't a lawsuit. Once the judge determined who was responsible for fixing the leak, that party would reimburse any expenses I'd incurred, as long as they were reasonable and I had the receipts: repairs, legal fees, medical fees, alternative housing.

The process is slow . . . but fair.

"Okay, let's do it." I told him if they debated the expert's decision, he should know now I wanted to push it to the judge. They weren't going to walk over this American. I had prejudice. I was the victim. I would be recompensed!

Before he could proceed, there was the little matter of reviewing the fees: his, about five thousand euros all told; the bailiff's, two hundred fifty euros; the expert's, seven thousand. My palms were sweating again, but he promised it would all be reimbursed.

What did people do who couldn't afford to lay out these fees to the courts? Did they just live with a leak until the walls caved in? I was lucky I had the resources, but I thought about my Parisian friends and their small salaries. What kind of a crazy system was this? Wasn't this a *socialist* country?

As we wrapped up our meeting, my young, cute lawyer gave me a long to-do list, including visits to a doctor and allergist, who would have to attest to my mold allergy.

It looked like I had a new full-time job.

Another day drew out, spent on my own. I'd tried some writing, even found a table in the sun at my favorite café on Boulevard Voltaire. Not much accomplished beyond a few paragraphs. It wasn't inspiration that was wanting; it was focus—I was still not used to the stillness of my days, the solitude. I didn't know how to be creative without the buzz of my colleagues around me. It was bad enough in New York, but not nearly as lonely as Paris was turning out to be.

I texted my Canadian neighbor, Andrea, to see if she wanted to meet me at the café for a drink after work. I'd hardly seen my friend since I arrived for this visit. She and I had always spent a lot of time together in the past.

"Sorry, I'm working on a big project!" came her reply.

This was the second invitation she'd turned down. The first time I reached out, her new boyfriend had been visiting from London. Her life had changed; she had other things to do.

In fact, most of my friends were less available than normal. I was spending days and nights on end alone. I wasn't used to this. Before, when I'd come to visit, my days would be filled with friends. It hadn't occurred to me that since I was in town for only a few days, my visit was an event. My friends rearranged their schedules to see me because I'd been away for months. But that wasn't going to be the day-to-day reality when I was here for a longer stretch.

It was going on three weeks of my being here, with several more ahead. My presence was no longer a novelty. After an initial surge of rendezvous, things tapered off as everyone settled back into his or her life. This was what living in Paris really felt like. It wouldn't have been so bad if I'd had a day job, as I used to, but the life of a writer was shaping up to be a solitary one. Walking around in my own head all the livelong day, I found I was a growing sick of myself. I'd wake up feeling heavy from too much me.

Maybe that was how Ma felt when we first moved to that one-horse town in New Jersey, her loneliness kicking up her self-loathing.

All this free time should have felt like an indulgence, an opportunity to do some real soul-searching, but I didn't want to search my soul. What if there was nothing going on in there worth finding?

Without my job, was I anybody? Did I matter anymore?

Around me, the café, where I sat looking at an empty page, was starting to fill with people for happy hour. The late afternoon sun begged to be enjoyed; I ached to have plans. Several more texts to friends went unanswered. I resigned myself to dinner alone at home, but refused to sulk about it, instead shopping at one of the Italian specialty stores on rue de Charonne for something special.

After all, I'd dined by myself at home in New York a lot during the work week, and it never felt anything but relaxed and homey.

Alone does not have to be lonely, I reminded myself.

Before turning onto my street, I popped in to see my *caviste*. A nice rosé would do me right. As would the sight of him.

He was in the stockroom again, so I called out. When he saw me, his eyes brightened. So did my disposition. He astonished me by kissing me hello on both cheeks.

"Helloooooo," he sang. "How are you?"

Was he a little buzzed? I heard laughter coming from the stockroom. "Whatta you got going on back there?"

He and some friends were having a drink. "It's my birthday!" he declared.

A perfect excuse for more cheek kisses. "Happy birthday!" And more cheek kisses. My efforts to cultivate a more personal relationship with my wine guy were paying off.

"We're going down to the river for a party on a boat," he said.

I wanted to do that! What a glorious way to spend a long summer night. I was envious of the fun they'd have, and jealous of his friends for being able to share in the fun with him. How many more pop-ins would it take, how many bottles of wine bought, before I'd get an invitation to join the party?

"Cheri!" I heard someone calling from the back, in a high falsetto. "Cheriiii! Where are youuuuu?"

A man emerged from the stockroom, long brown hair, full beard. His thin, muscular body was squeezed into a dress, his feet into white stilettos. Around his neck: an acid-green feather boa. "Oops!" he said, hand to his mouth. "Sorry! You have a client!" He pranced back to the stockroom, giggling.

Oh. Hmm.

"My friends are crazy," my *caviste* said, shaking his head.

Were they going to a costume party? Was this just silly frat boy antics, or . . . ? *Cheri, where are you!*

Crap.

So much for my new husband. I bought my wine and shuffled home. Damn. I knew he was just a little too pretty.

I poured myself a big glass of rosé. Preparing dinner for one didn't feel homey anymore. Alone became lonely again.

A text from Fabien popped up on my phone. "Do you want to have dinner on my terrace tonight?"

Thank God! I wrapped the food back up and grabbed the bottle of wine, along with some dessert. Fabien always seemed to know when I needed to be rescued from myself. Dinner for one? Not tonight.

"I don't think he's gay," Fabien consoled me as he set the table on his large terrace—a bonus that came with his bitty two-hundred-square-foot studio. Seven floors up and facing west, the terrace afforded views of Place de la Bastille and the Eiffel Tower. The sun was still an hour from setting, but already the sky was growing rosy.

"But what about the guy in drag?" I asked, following Fabien back inside to the kitchen, sipping my wine. My host didn't drink, but that wasn't stopping me.

Fabien tossed a salad of rich green leaves dotted with lentils and quinoa. "It's kale. Just for you." Before coming to stay in Paris, Land of Breads and Cheeses, I ate kale every day. Lately, though, my jeans were fitting a bit more snugly. Not enough kale.

Fabien started for the terrace again, salad bowl in hand. "Bring the bread."

"But how do you know he's not gay?" I asked, trailing him with the basket of sliced baguette.

Fabien shrugged. "When we went there before I didn't get a feeling." He struck a match and lit four tea lights on the table. "Look at the sky!"

The sun had dropped closer to the horizon, intensifying the colors: orange, crimson, and purple.

"You didn't get the gay vibe?"

"No." Fabien dished out the salad. "By the way, I also made a Spanish tortilla!"

Tortilla, nice, fine—whatever! Could we get back to that green feather boa? "But what about the drag queen?"

"I don't know."

"How can you *not* know?" He hadn't gotten the gay vibe from the *caviste*, but he couldn't explain the man in the dress? "You need to go back there and make sure. See if he flirts with you. I gotta know!" Why was I grasping so hard at a man I barely knew? Did I feel rejected by him before we'd even really interacted? Pre-rejected?

There was my mother looking in the ugly mirror again.

"Don't worry," Fabien said. "Enjoy the beautiful sky."

Fabien was making me anxious. How dare he be blithe about my plight. Didn't he care? Didn't I matter? *Fine, I'll look at the stupid sky.* It was changing by the minute—the lower the sun sank, the more intense and beautiful the outcome. Maybe there was a lesson there, something about good things coming out of endings.

After we ate our salad, Fabien cleared the plates, returning from the kitchen with the parfaits I'd brought from Picard Surgelés, a favorite Parisian shop, the last word—*le dernier cris*—in frozen gourmet foods. Even the most chic Parisians bought Picard apéritifs for their cocktail parties. My apartment had a Picard a block away, which I was pretty sure raised my property value.

"What about Serge?" Fabien asked me as he set the desserts down, a demitasse spoon beside each.

Serge? "Who the hell is that?"

"The waiter from the tapas place."

His name was Serge? I just remembered him as that sweet, chubby guy with huge brown puppy eyes and a wicked sense of humor. For whatever reason, that waiter made my heart pound. My friends and I kept going back to the tapas place where he worked—four days in a row—just so I could see him. But I chickened out before I could seal the deal. Then I went back to New

York and put him out of my mind. Prerejected myself. It's easier that way, isn't it?

"He flirt a lot with you last times." Fabien's eyes glinted in the candlelight. "He likes you, I think."

He likes me? Huh. Well, to hell with the sexually ambiguous wine seller. I'd go with the low-hanging fruit. Tapas, anyone?

"Look, Liza!" Fabien pointed at the horizon to the west.

The sun had disappeared below the skyline, lighting the fringes of the city on fire, turning the sky above it a deep blue velvet. In the distance, the Eiffel Tower sparkled.

Maybe I didn't have a man in my life, but Paris would provide enough romance for now. It was my one constant and true love, even though it had sprung a leak *chez moi*. But as they say, with French lovers, you have to put up with some slaps along with the strokes.

We'd see about Serge. Maybe I didn't really care one way or another. After all, I was just starting to get it together on my own.

"Ma! Ma!"

I was gasping for air, my bronchial tubes tightening. No. Not again.

Shooting up in bed, I cried out, "Ma!" It took everything I had. I coughed hard. My chest wheezed and rattled.

"I'm here, baby girl."

My mother appeared at my door, a bottle of medicine in one hand, a glass of water in the other. She flicked on the light beside my bed, illuminating her face, a vision of calm and confidence. "It's okay. I'm here."

I was eight years old and having asthma attacks nearly every week.

Ma gave me a spoonful of Myrax, a new miracle drug that tasted of orange, but with a cloying base that made me gag every time. My mother always had a water chaser ready. Seconds later, the attack ceased.

"Blessed relief," Ma said, handing me the glass of water. "Right, baby girl?"

I took a sip, nodded. "Better."

I was diagnosed with asthma when I was in second grade. My great-grandmother died of it, after plucking chickens for a big family dinner. We were both allergic to birds, among other things.

At an allergy clinic a few towns away from my home, they poked me with dozens of needles to test for allergies and help find the possible sources of the asthma. A week later, my mother and I sat in the allergist's consulting room as he listed nearly twenty allergens, including eggs, which I adored, as well as mold, dust, pollen, birds, dogs, and cats.

"Cats?" I asked.

"Very strong," my doctor replied.

Ma glanced at me, then the doctor. "But we have a cat."

The doctor pressed his lips together for a moment. "Unless you get rid of the cat, your daughter's attacks will continue."

Not Kitty! No! A single tear trickled from my right eye. We had to get rid of Kitty because of me? My sister was going to hate me. This was a nightmare.

"And no stuffed animals," the doctor added. "Not near the bed at night."

My stuffed animals, too? But I'd had them ever since I could remember. They were birthday presents from friends, Christmas presents from aunts. They were my friends who kept me safe at night.

"Curtains aren't a good idea, either," the doctor said. "If they're near the bed. You need to strip her room down to the essentials."

Well, that wasn't fair. Maria got to have a girly room with stuffed animals and ruffled swag curtains. And what would my friend Christine think when she came over and the only thing in my room was a bed and a shade covering the window? She'd make fun of me, that's what. Her room was pink and perfect, and had shag carpeting.

Why me? I was cursed. This was horrible.

I cried harder.

"Don't worry, baby girl," Ma said. "We won't get rid of Kitty." She asked the doctor if they could do something for me so we could keep our beloved tabby.

"Well," the doctor said, cocking his head, "if you're not willing to get rid of the cat, she'll need shots every week."

"Every week?" my mother asked. "How many?"

"We don't know yet, but we'll focus on her worst allergies, the ones she can't avoid."

"I can take shots," I offered. "I can do that." It was the least I could do so we could keep Kitty—and I could be normal.

Doctors' visits were routine for me starting at two years old, when I was hospitalized for weeks with whooping cough, pneumonia, and croup. I remember being under a tent, the worry in my mother's eyes. I also remember being furious once they finally freed me from that place.

"You were such a little brat after you got out," Ma would later say. "Poor baby."

Well, yeah. They'd abandoned me there, hadn't they?

Respiratory illness was a regular part of my life, ever since I was born with fluid in my lungs. Every fall, bronchitis would grab hold. It got worse each year, until second grade, when I was out of school for nearly a month. That's when the asthma started.

Some spiritualists say different emotions lodge in certain organs, creating illness. The lungs, as it turns out, are the site of grief. While my mother was pregnant with me, she was going through some tough family issues. "I cried every day," she said, though she never elaborated on what the issues were about. Did her grief transfer to me, her unborn child? Was this why I came into the world with fluid in my lungs?

Was carrying my mother's grief and pain something born in me, why I felt so responsible for fixing it?

Despite ten years of trips to the allergist every Friday for three shots in both arms, my asthma would rob me of my ability to run around with my friends in the crisp autumn air; stop me from playing on the first girls' soccer team in high school, after helping to form the squad.

But then, I was never really an athletic kid; I was an artist, a musician. I started doing plays at the local theater in town, and that was fine with me.

My health and allergies improved when I moved to New York, "where nothing grows," as my mother used to say. "The city is the best thing for you."

Both my parents were born and grew up in Buffalo. At that time, it was surrounded by mills and smelting plants. My parents met at the chemical company where they both worked, where women received a special allowance for stockings because the air was so thick with acids that their stockings would pit as they walked across campus. They took this for granted.

My parents hated country life. My illness born of our natural surroundings only fueled their arguments against "the middle of nowhere" we lived in.

Would my allergies have vastly improved if we'd given Kitty away? Most definitely. I suffered terribly because of her. But we kept her until her death, which came when I was in art school in New York.

I always thought Ma kept Kitty for her children's sake, but years later she commented, "There was no way I was going to give Kitty away—as long as we could give you shots."

I wasn't sure if she really meant it; Ma was always blurting out things like that. I preferred to think of her as the woman at my bedroom door with the cure for my ailment, saying, "I'm here, baby girl." Because she was always there when I needed her.

It had been twenty years since I had an asthma attack, but here I was, gasping for air in a doctor's office near the swanky Parc Monceau in the 8th arrondissement.

Thanks to my leak, I had not only a lawyer in Paris, but also a doctor—a nice Englishwoman recommended to me by an expat friend. When you're sick in a foreign country, you don't want a single *fawfaw* getting in the way of your getting well.

I had explained my leaky situation, listed all my symptoms.

"But you say they dissipate after twenty minutes spent outside your apartment?"

"Yes, except the asthma." Because once those tubes shut, you can't pry them open without drugs. I knew that all too well.

"Okay, I'll write this up for your lawyer," my new doctor said. "But you'll need some meds to cope with your symptoms."

Yes, please.

She listed five different drugs as she typed them into her computer: an inhaler for immediate relief, another with longer-lasting effects, a nose spray for the sinus inflammation, drops for the burning eyes, and an antihistamine pill to keep the symptoms at bay. "You really should get out of there, though," she said. "Is there anywhere else you can stay?"

Yeah, New York, but that was not an option. I'd gone through so much finally to be here in Paris; I wasn't going to leave now, asthma or no.

"I understand what you're going through," she said. "We had a leak in our apartment."

Her, too?

"The neighbor's washing machine," she said. "It flooded our living room. We still can't get the mold out." Her friend with a mold allergy couldn't visit anymore. "Paris is a very damp city. It's hard to get rid of mold—and it's everywhere."

Well, that's just great. Paris: one big mold spore.

She printed out the scripts on a letter-size piece of paper, divided in two, with everything listed twice. "This half is for the pharmacist," she said, indicating, "and this is for you."

She promised me that the drugs would greatly improve my

symptoms. "But if not, just call me. I'll get the letter to your lawyer by the end of the week."

The visit cost a fraction of what a New York doctor would have charged—and that was the fee for nonresidents. The prescription drugs also cost next to nothing compared to the States. Maybe the average Frenchman couldn't afford a lawyer to fight his leak problem, but at least the meds to fight the effects of it were cheap.

You couldn't change your lot in life, but the suffering would be made tolerable. *Vive la France!*

"You can't stay there," Sarah said. We were having dinner in one of my haunts near rue Saint Maur. "You can barely breathe. Let me help you find somewhere else." She was in real estate; she had resources.

I had drugs; I was fine. Plus, I'd just unpacked three suitcases of clothes I'd spent three weeks buying expressly for this trip. My cabinet was full of toiletries, my cupboard stocked with my favorite foods. I was installed in my apartment—physically *and* emotionally.

Don't make me leave.

I'd come all this way finally to live in my neighborhood. I didn't want to give up that dream. This was the point of having my own place. How could I walk away now?

"It's up to you," she said, "but you don't sound good."

Others offered, too. An expat friend owned a small apartment in Montmartre whose tenant had quit on the lease. I'd loved Montmartre since my first visit when I was sixteen. Might it be fun to live there awhile?

But, no, I dug in my heels. I wanted to stay near my friends, to write in my favorite café on Boulevard Voltaire. No, no, no!

Then Sarah emailed me about an apartment on Île de la Cité, near Notre Dame, in the heart of the city. It was a large one-bedroom in a historic seventeenth-century building—vacant until September 1.

I was being handed an apartment just when I needed it. Sarah was right: my home was making me sick. How much was I willing to suffer to stay there?

Or maybe the better question was *why* was I willing to suffer to stay there?

An hour later, Fabien and I were standing on Quai aux Fleurs, on the bank of the Seine, waiting for Sarah's agent to show me the apartment near Notre Dame. While we waited, I looked across the river toward Hôtel de Ville—Paris City Hall—its windows gleaming hot in the afternoon sun. The leaves of the linden trees along the river shimmered in the breeze.

The 4th arrondissement was beautiful, no doubt. Desirable, too. This could be a chance to live in an area of the city I couldn't normally afford.

But tourists owned the place in summer. I hadn't come to Paris to live like a tourist, had I?

The agent arrived, and we descended from the quay to a narrow street no wider than an alley: rue des Chantres—Street of the Cantors. Fabien wasted no time pointing out the significance of the street name to his friend the singer.

This cool, quiet lane led to another, just as quaint, the kind of quaint that makes tourists swoon. We walked past ancient two-story homes, some of whose façades dripped with wisteria.

I thought of my mother, how much she'd have loved this.

We came to a building with a plain white plaster façade, its large carriage door studded with ancient nail heads. Just in front, a row of parked motorcycles, or *motos*. Fabien grabbed my arm, poked his finger at the headquarters of the motorcycle brigade for the French National Police, just across the street. Four young cops in leather chaps stood outside.

Fabien darted his wide eyes at me. "You have to live here," he said under his breath.

I shook my head. "Stop it, you. We haven't seen the place yet."

"Who cares?" The more excited he grew, the higher his voice. "It's perfect!"

The agent pressed a brass button on the front of the building, and the door clicked open, revealing a cobbled courtyard. Ivy clung to the interior. The door closed behind us, shutting out the modern world and the city beyond. Suddenly we were in a haven in the countryside, far away from the tourist fracas all around.

The apartment was on the far side of the courtyard, up a flight of stone stairs worn thin from three hundred years of climbing feet. Fabien and I exchanged glances, our eyes echoing each other's sentiments: this was a rare opportunity.

The door of the apartment swung open on heavy iron hinges, which looked centuries old. Fabien squeezed my hand as we entered.

Impeccably renovated with ten-foot-high ceilings, the apartment had windows facing two courtyards on either side, letting in air and light. It had a small but fully equipped kitchen, better than mine in New York and certainly better than the one in my place in the 11th arrondissement. Again, I felt my hand being squeezed.

In the bedroom, a writing desk faced a small terrace.

This tipped Fabien over the edge. "It's amazing! You have to take it!"

Yes, it was wonderful, but not as sunny as my apartment, and I was still hung up on the touristy district: the souvenir shops, the overpriced, mediocre cafés. This wasn't the way I wanted to live in Paris, was it? The city was home to me now, and I wanted it to feel like it.

As if to open myself to the idea of the place, I flung open the seven-foot-tall window facing the courtyard. A breeze ruffled the ivy, transforming it into a vertical sea, waves of changing shades of green. A single church bell chimed, its high, clear tone vibrating in the air. Another bell chased the vibrations of the first. Then another, a deeper bong. Then more and more bells, each deeper and louder than the last, until the apartment filled with what seemed like hundreds of bells. A celebration of bells.

"That's your mama!" Fabien said. "She wants you to be here."

The bells of Notre Dame pealed for more than seven minutes. I listened, looking out at the rustling ivy, tears welling. *Ma wants you here.*

"Okay. I'll take it."

It took three weeks of shopping and planning to put together my outfits for Paris. I had a whole theme going: Parisian Summer Chic. This look required three purses, four jackets, six skirts, seven pairs of pants, twelve tops, and fifteen pairs of shoes. Just the essentials. Everything had been pressed and hung by color, the shoes lined up from my low-top sneakers to my platforms.

I'd been staring at my clothes for ten minutes unable to make a decision—not about what to wear, but what to take to the apartment on Île de la Cité. I shouldn't take it all, should I? Was I really up to hauling three suitcases across town? It seemed like overkill for just a few weeks, and the thought of packing everything up again after I'd just hung it, all nice and organized, made me want to weep.

Still, the thought of being without anything was worse, especially after all the trouble I'd gone through to bring it here. It was just another plan foiled by the leak.

No, I'd bring just the basics—some favorite pieces and a few pairs of shoes. That was the reasonable thing to do.

Narrowing it down to the "basics" was agonizing. I needed it all. I wanted it all. My stuff! My stuff! I'd fondle something that didn't make the cut, sigh, and hang it back. What a waste. Thirty minutes later and I was still debating, growing more and more anxious. What if the one thing I really needed were left behind? How could I be sure I was making the right decisions?

Jeezuz, Lisa, it's just clothing! What was wrong with me?

I went through the same agony over the toiletries and food-stuffs. Even if I'd moved the whole show to the new venue—three suitcases in all—it wouldn't have felt any better. I'd still be leaving my home behind.

An hour later, I'd packed the smallest suitcase with some essentials and a shopping tote of toiletries and perishable foods, including an opened bottle of wine.

It was still plenty heavy. I lugged it all on the Métro during the crush of rush hour. Bad idea. My fellow riders stared at me, shook their heads. I was in their way.

At Hôtel de Ville station, I had to heave all of it up the stairs, slog it over the bridge to Île de la Cité, and drag it to the apartment building, stumbling over the cobblestones that just yesterday seemed so freaking charming.

Inside the apartment, I dumped everything in the middle of the living room floor and then collapsed on the bed.

If I'm living the dream, somebody, please wake me.

Thirteen

Living in Exile

I woke up in a strange bed, in a strange apartment. I rose, groggy, my feet moving me into the living room, slapping on the cold parquet.

The bells of Notre Dame struck ten.

My luggage was where I'd left it, in the middle of the living room, but at some point the night before I had put the perishables in the refrigerator—with the exception of the wine. That, I polished off sitting at the small dining table, looking out at the pigeons kicking up a fuss in the ivy—fighting, or doing "it," or whatever. Anyway, they'd had more fun than I.

There were clothes that had to be dealt with. It comforted me that the closet was a good size and stocked with nearly two dozen hangers and four deep shelves. The little things went a long way. It was a nice apartment, for sure; I needed to have gratitude about that. In time.

Right now, I was looking out at heavy, gray clouds rolling in and lamenting the scarves I'd left at home.

I ate a yogurt standing at the kitchen sink. Halfway through the bowl, I reminded myself to savor it, my favorite flavor found only in Paris, what I'd waited two months to enjoy again: rhubarb.

A cup of tea. A warm shower. The bells of Notre Dame struck eleven.

The clouds brought the cold and damp with them. I zipped my jacket tight around my neck as I stepped outside. Goose bumps popped up over my bare legs. The display on my phone told me it was fifty-seven degrees, in August.

The queue for the bell tower of Notre Dame wrapped around the entire garden to Quai de l'Archevêché. Tourist families huddled together for warmth, undaunted by the weather. I thought of Ma, how every vacation had to include a visit to somewhere historic—Williamsburg, Gettysburg. All those endless lines we waited on, the plaques she read aloud to us in a voice choked with emotion.

Did those tourists appreciate the history around them or was this just something to be checked off the to-do list? Did they know how lucky they were to have each other?

I walked along the river, moving at the pace of someone with purpose, but it was just muscle memory from my former life. I told myself to slow down, look around. There was nowhere to be.

But I didn't know how to be nowhere.

Tension gripped my shoulders, my neck ached, my chest tightened. *It's the cold,* I told myself. I had to buy a scarf, but all I could find were souvenir shops.

"What you want, lady?" a man at one of the shops asked me in pidgin English.

"Scarf."

He indicated a rack of long cottony scarves imprinted with some kind of a pattern. "Five euros."

I whipped one off the rack without looking, sending the display spinning round and round, the tails of the scarves flying in the air.

"You want something else?" the man asked, shaking a large metal ring of Eiffel Tower key chains. "For you, lady, three for seven—"

"Just the scarf." I thrust my five-euro bill at him and dashed off.

"I'm not a tourist," I said to no one and everyone, stuffing the scarf in my purse.

Tourists clogged the sidewalk, so I crossed to the quay side. They clogged that side, too. I gave up and moved into the interior of the island, meandering through the green stalls of the bird and plant market near police headquarters. A parakeet screeched in its cage, flapping its wings, white, green, and black. I resisted an urge to open its cage door to see if it would free itself.

A group of young policemen, fit like soldiers, walked past wearing riot gear. Their stony faces warned against flirtation.

Another endless queue of tourists lined Boulevard du Palais, waiting to see Saint-Chapelle, which sat trapped for a few hundred years inside the Palais de Justice complex. I'd never seen it. One day—but not today.

Back on the quay, I walked past the Conciergerie, dazzling white after they'd scrubbed decades of soot from the stone façade. They'd left a tiny, sooty patch so you wouldn't forget the past. I took a picture of it.

I looked out at the Seine, at the glass-top barges stuffed with tourists snapping photos of the Conciergerie and me, their phones aloft, creating a wall between themselves and the real thing.

The damp air forced me finally to pull out the scarf wadded up in my purse: pink and white, with famous Paris monuments on it. I am not a tourist. I twisted it, obscuring the monuments and my embarrassment, and wrapped it around my neck. Tacky, but warm.

Across the river, on the embankment, the Paris Plages was deserted, its blue beach umbrellas closed up tight. No sun today for the artificial beach. How optimistic the Parisians were in July, when they built their Riviera on the Seine—dreams of picnics, bathing beauties, and volleyball. But August would leave everyone cold.

Such a shame, I thought. Such a waste.

I looked away, walked farther up the quay. A feeling of futility gripped me. So much beauty around me, but it felt empty. Maybe the tourists had cast this veil of melancholy over me. Or the touristy veneer on everything in this district—all charm but no heart. Theme Park Paris.

Maybe it felt empty because it was empty—of Parisians, abandoning their city for the August vacation, leaving it to the tourists, who'd moved in and taken over.

Like on the Pont des Arts. Tourists scrambled over it, scrawling graffiti, hanging padlocks on the wire mesh siding. It barely resembled its former self, disfigured by the weight of trite tourist sentiment clinging six inches thick on the parapets, ripping the wire meshing from its frame.

I stood in the middle of the bridge, the veil of melancholy drawing in tighter, toward my gut, twisting up my insides.

I recalled the first time I'd come here, with a man I was crazy about. He held my hand for the first time as we crossed the bridge, which was transparent then, ethereal, like walking on the water. We sat on one of the benches, looked out at the Pont Neuf, talking until daylight crept up around the edges of the city.

I had to fight to hold the memory in my mind because that bridge was gone, and the one I was standing on had a view only of metal and plywood sprayed with graffiti.

No one seemed to care about the ugliness they were creating. They went on smiling, destroying something I loved. It had been perfect, and now that was gone. *Ugly.*

"Saboteurs," I heard myself say.

The tourists took no notice of me. They just kept hanging their padlocks and snapping their photos, oblivious of the pain they were causing. I wanted to push their faces into the wall of locks and tell them to wake up. *You're doing this!* I was shaking with rage. *You're killing it!*

My mind flashed on the bubbling wall of my apartment; my mother in her hospice bed.

I wept into my scarf of beautiful Paris monuments.

Well, at least I knew what was really bothering me.

I kept a folder of notes from Ma. Little, insignificant jottings that had been attached to articles she'd send in the mail, or to a birthday check. "Here you go, baby girl. Deposit right away!"

If the notes came around Halloween, she'd sign with a jack-o'-lantern drawing. Easter, a cross and lily, or a bunny. One of my favorites was a homemade tag she'd taped to a box of Valentine candy hearts. She fashioned a piece of note paper into a heart and cut fringe all around. "Love you so, so, so, so, so, so much!" it read in red ink. Then, "Mama."

Love you so, so, so, so, so, so much. This was one of the last things she said to me, but something she had said often, either on the phone or as I was leaving after a weekend visit. Always six sos.

I took photos of all Ma's notes before I left for Paris, kept them on my phone to read when I needed to hear from her.

I needed them a lot these days.

One note was not originally meant for me. My sister and I found it tacked to the side of her refrigerator when we were cleaning out the house. Neatly printed on a folded piece of paper, she'd copied down a saying from one of her prayer books no doubt, a mantra for her day: The peace of God is at the core of my being. I am serene.

My mother had been spinning inside, too. Like her daughter—never resting, never finding peace. She could never just be happy in the moment, or at least not for a sustained period of time. Something always nagged at her—a noise, a draft, something left undone.

And of course the unknowns were her biggest concerns.

"What if something happens to you in that apartment when you're all alone?" she asked me one night when I was having dinner at her house.

"What's going to happen?" I asked, crunching on a crispy roast potato.

"You could fall in the shower. They'd never find you all alone in there."

I assured her that eventually the smell would alert the neighbors, and the super would discover my body.

"That's not funny!" she said, pointing her forkful of chicken at me. "It happens all the time."

"I hope you don't stay up nights worrying about that, Ma. Falling in the shower? So cliché." There was probably a greater chance I'd get hit by a bus, anyway. And that would put me conveniently out in the street, where everyone would find me. "Am I supposed to buy one of those call alert things? I mean, come on. You need that more than I do."

She complained that those were for old people. Even when she was eighty, Ma referred to people her age as "those old people," as if unaware of her own aging—or maybe as a way to ward off her mortality.

"I'm just worried about you in that big city on your own," she continued. "I hope you chain your door at night."

"Yeah, but then the super can't get in to rescue me if something happens."

Losing power in a rainstorm, entering traffic circles, the leaves clogging the gutters—worry and fear clouded every minute of my mother's day. She was always prepared for any problem that might arise, her purse containing any possible thing we might need, from meds to a sewing kit. Just-in-case Mommy, I called her. It was her way of coping with the scary unknowns. I am the same; my ability to worry in advance of potential problems, and plan for them, is probably what makes me a great creative director. But as a way to live? Not so happy-making.

I didn't know how to be serene, either, always poised for the buzz kill. Surely it was coming; it was just a matter of time. Bad things always happened. Nothing stayed good forever. This is what I learned from Ma.

"We always have crappy luck," she would say, as if our family were cursed. "Just once, it would be nice if we could get a break." This was why it was useless to play the lottery. We weren't meant to win those things. Of course, if you believe in luck, then say we're plumb out of it, life gets fatalistic pretty fast.

According to Ma's way of thinking, we were doomed. At that point, any chance of serenity was slim.

When the bad things Ma feared came to pass, she'd say God was punishing her.

"I think He hates me."

"Really, Ma? You? Why?"

"I'm not a very nice person."

She hung on to the idea that bad luck and illness were God's way of sticking it to her for pissing him off.

"Your God's kinda mean," I joked. I always poked fun at her when she talked this way because it had to be made as ridiculous as possible, or it might seep into me and become a part of my thinking, too.

Or was it too late?

The peace of God is at the core of my being. I am serene.

It saddens me to think my mother was so troubled, that she may have lived her entire life never having known real peace of mind. But there's nothing I can do about that.

On the day she died, my mother never looked more beautiful. Her face was completely relaxed and smooth of any lines. Whatever worry had tugged on it over the years had finally let go, and on that final day of her life, perhaps peace came at last.

I wanted to find that same peace now—while I was still very much alive and in the prime of my life—but being my mother's daughter, it was a struggle every day, especially with everything I was going through here in Paris. Fighting for peace—was that the right way to look at it, or was there another way to find serenity and happiness?

"Where u?"

My contractor, Aiden, texted me.

"Île de la Cité." Sitting at the table watching the pigeons frolicking in the ivy for the second day in a row. In front of me, an open document in my writing program, the curser blinking on the same blank page for the last hour.

"Meet us. Drinks. Rue des Archives."

Aiden and I had started hanging out socially after we discovered we had mutual friends. My serious, hardworking contractor turned out to be a hell of a lot of fun after he'd hung up his hammer for the day. He and some of our friends were just across the bridge from my temporary digs, offering a cure for my malaise. But I needed to keep writing.

The curser blinked, waiting for me to fill the page. Blinked and blinked. Outside my window, the ivy turned deep green in the waning afternoon light. Lonely curser. Lonely me. Blink. Blink. Blink.

"Be there in five minutes."

"Hurry missy. Ordered our second round."

Rue des Archives overflowed with people, like a block party. I found Aiden and some of our friends drinking pints of beer outside one of the bars, standing at tall pub tables designed for that purpose. But others who could not find an available table simply hung out on the sidewalk or stood in the street, chatting with beers in hand. In New York, we'd have been fined for drinking in public.

It didn't matter that it was Sunday and most people had to work the next day; everyone was out, filling the cafés lining the street. When it came to life's pleasures, Paris had it all over my other city.

The malaise of the day lifted.

This was my favorite time of day—the apéritif hour, or *apéro*—that magic time between lunch and dinner that created yet another excuse to drink, eat, and hang out with friends. It was also the reason you could find cafés packed every day from five to eight in the evening, when in New York they'd be dead. I loved this time, because no matter what my friends had planned for the evening, I could usually find someone to have a glass of wine with for at least a few hours before another evening of solitude kicked in.

"I'm so glad you texted," I said. "I hit a wall with my writing."

"Not good," Aiden said, furrowing his brow. "You need to stay focused, missy." Then he put a pint of beer in front of me, which advised the opposite.

"You need a hot romance to spice up your book," he said. "Whatever happened with the waiter?"

"Serge."

Fabien and I had gone to the restaurant three times. I fell for Serge all over again—his sweet, humble mannerisms, his shy smile, and that impish glint in the corner of his eye that said there was something else under all that sweet shyness. When he and I got to talking about my blog, I finally seized the opportunity to give him my card. Serge blushed when I handed it to him, but promised to contact me. Fabien congratulated me on landing my future husband.

"He never called," I told Aiden. "It's been two weeks. I think he's married."

He told me that didn't stop a guy in Paris.

"I'm nobody's mistress," I said. "It's a bust. I've moved on."

"What about your sexy *caviste*?"

I relayed the tale of the mysterious man in drag whom I'd encountered on my last visit to the wine shop. "But Fabien said I should still go for it."

One of our friends, Thierry, was shaking his head.

"You sure?" I asked him. "But my friend didn't get the vibe. And he's gay."

Thierry just kept shaking his head, his lips pursed. "Sorry. Doesn't look good."

So much for my hot, romantic plot line.

More friends joined us as others parted. We ordered another round.

Aiden asked me how I liked the apartment on Île de la Cité.

Turned out, he'd worked on the renovation project with an architect friend. "It's really nice, isn't it?"

I nodded. "And I can breathe in it."

As soon as Aiden and I started talking about my leak, others in our group chimed in with their own experiences, like fish stories, each saying theirs was bigger. *My entire ceiling came down on me while I was sleeping . . . Me, I lived with a hole in my wall for three years until things dried out . . .*

You would think hearing I wasn't alone in my plight would have been a comfort.

You would be wrong.

"It's an old city, Lisa," Aiden said. "Things leak."

So this was the real reason everyone hung out in bars drinking. No one wanted to go home to their leaks.

The sun finally pushed its way through the gray clouds, bathing us in a red-orange hue, having its last hurrah before it quit for the night. We polished off another round.

"Dinnertime?" Aiden asked.

My spinning head told me it was dinnertime an hour ago. "Please."

We grabbed another of our friends, Antoine, and our threesome fell into a place just up the street that had a retro-American-diner theme. Yet another café with a retro-American-diner theme. This, and anything Brooklyn-esque, was the new trend, much to my horror. I usually avoided these places because I wasn't living in Paris to eat in Brooklyn, U.S.A.

Buried in my menu, I didn't notice the waiter come to our table.

"Tell me!" was all he said. *Dites-moi!*

I looked up to see a face smiling at me, all teeth and cheekbones. Another café, another waiter to crush hard on. This one had low-slung jeans hanging on his slim waist and a tattoo on one of his sinewy forearms.

"How can I satisfy you?" he asked me, still smiling.

I looked to Aiden. "Did he say—"

"Yup."

I wasn't going to touch that one.

The waiter asked us if we were English—in perfect English. Aiden explained our United Nations of a group: French, South African, American.

"New York," I qualified, as if that might make me somehow cooler.

"Ah, New York! Cool!" said the tattooed waiter right on cue, in a French accent so imperceptible it almost diminished his sexiness. Almost.

"I'm staying here two months," I added. *Plenty of time to get to know me*, I implied, hoping to inspire Cupid to shoot his arrow.

"That's great," he said. "I hope you will come here often."

Target acquired.

"Lisa's a writer," Aiden touted. "She's in Paris to write her masterpiece."

The waiter's eyes brightened. "Impressive," he said. "You should come here and write."

Somewhere in there we managed to order our food, but not before we found a way to flirt, too, about everything from the wine he suggested to the burger I ordered.

"He sure likes *you*," Aiden said after the waiter left to put in our order. "He barely looked at us."

I was pretty sure the waiter was just being French, but Antoine saw it differently and said so with a few *fawfaws*.

"Antoine says the guy's definitely smitten," Aiden translated. "So, you need to work that, missy."

"He's probably twenty-five," I said. "Maybe thirty. *Maybe*."

"So what! Men aren't about age here. And *you* look thirty!"

Antoine nodded.

"Go for it. You still got it," Aiden said.

Go for it. Should I? The last time I tried, it backfired. "Men don't like aggressive women here."

Antoine gave me advice on love, French-style, while Aiden translated. In France, it wasn't about being coy; it was about subtlety—and timing. He thought our waiter friend was primed. All I needed to do was give him a sign I was interested and nothing more. It was enough for now. "Make him think about it." Leave him wanting. Then, maybe a week later, return. Repeat the process as needed.

Much the same as getting leaks fixed, the process for l'amour in Paris seemed unnecessarily drawn out.

It was a busy night at the café, so we didn't see our waiter much after the initial exchange. We left our money on the table and walked out.

"Excuse me! Miss!" I heard someone call out. "Miss!"

Our waiter came running out of the restaurant. I instinctively searched for my cell phone, thinking I'd left it behind.

"I wanted to say good-bye," he said. "My name is Leo—Léon in French. What's your name?"

He repeated my name after I told him, his almond eyes studying my face. "I'm so happy to meet you."

Serge, who? "Do you prefer Leo, or Léon?"

"Well . . . Léon is my real name."

"Then I'll call you that."

His face went red. Antoine was right: he did seem smitten. "I hope you come back." Then he told me his entire schedule for the week.

And the week after.

Yeah, I still got it.

I walked home bathed in the glow of the lights of Hôtel de Ville. The Seine reflected the lights back at me. The clouds had rolled away, revealing a blanket of stars and a round moon, larger than I'd ever seen.

Oh, Paris, my love, how could I have forgotten how wonderful you are?

———

I had nothing but time to enjoy Paris.

For once, I walked right past my favorite store, the BHV. There was no pressing reason to go today. I had tomorrow. Or the next day.

Paris without an agenda. I told myself it was a luxury to be able to take the city in long strides—days bleeding together, life on an endless conveyor belt, always moving forward, bringing another opportunity to do something. Or nothing, if I so chose.

But if I did nothing, guilt ensued.

I was still uneasy in my unstructured life, still making schedules: *Today I'll go to the Latin Quarter, tomorrow Saint-Germain-des-Prés.* I was wound up tight inside, my former life still setting the pace.

And I needed to be busy to evade the malaise.

It rained every day, the cold and damp seeping into my bones, wearing me down. Water, dampness, a pervasive theme since I'd arrived. I was missing a beautiful summer in New York and starting to resent Paris for robbing me of the few warm months of the year.

Why couldn't I just be happy? Did I even know how?

I was living the dream in Paris. I owed it to my colleagues, my friends, to dreamers everywhere, to be elated every day. Didn't I?

I couldn't shake the gloom, the fear and loathing. The loneliness. Paris was supposed to be my happy place, but now it was turning on me.

Or was it me?

I thought when I left my job back in New York and took the leap to come to Paris, it would feel incredible, fulfilling. Taking huge, bold steps should be rewarding. When you climb the mountain, you're supposed to embrace the view, the new perspective. You're supposed to yell, "Woohoo!" into the air.

I just felt stranded on the mountain. It's lonely work, blazing a trail.

All your life, they encourage you to dream big. "Reach for the stars," they tell children. But no one ever said anything about how you'd feel after the dream became real. You grew up thinking that once you were living the dream, all your problems would be solved. You'd be magically transformed into an untouchable, celestial being living happily ever after.

Instead, you're still you, lugging around all the same crap—the same fears, the same self-doubt. A black-and-white Dorothy in a Technicolor Oz.

From the open window of the apartment, I could hear Notre Dame's bells tolling every fifteen minutes, eking out its melody until the top of the hour, when it would play the whole tune and bong the time. As those bells bonged my day away, I grew more anxious.

Ding-dang-dong! Sun is shining finally!

Ding-dang-dong-ding! It's two-thirty!

Ding-dang-dong-ding—dang, girl! Why are you still inside?

I'd had the whole day planned. I was going to the café of my tattooed waiter, Léon, to "write" until his shift ended. Then he would, I hoped, invite me for a postwork drink, and maybe dinner. It was Paris; anything was possible.

Then the self-loathing kicked in.

My steady diet of brioche, cheese, and wine had taken effect. Everything in the closet was tight. Two, three, four outfit changes, and nothing looked good. Clothes were chucked all over on the floor. I thought of all the things left behind in my apartment in my own neighborhood that might have worked. And what about the changeable weather? Did I need the leather jacket, or would that be too hot? Were any of my sexy shoes waterproof? I spun and spun, unable to commit. What if I'd regret it later?

I hated when I got like this. A meltdown was imminent.

Ding-dang-dong-ding! Dong-dang-ding-dong! shamed the bells of Notre Dame as they chimed three o'clock.

The sun shifted beyond the courtyard; the apartment grew dark. I was losing a rare sunny day in this cold, rainy August. If I missed it, I'd feel more alone than ever by the time evening came. *What the hell is wrong with you, moron? You're pathetic!* I screamed at myself in my head. My personal pep talks had never been of the "Go, girl! You can do it!" variety. Not surprising, considering I didn't exactly grow up in the house of self-nurturing. I was always the mean gym teacher to my dorky, awkward eight-year-old self who was still getting picked last for teams.

But the self-shaming worked in this case. I got over myself, got dressed, and got out of the apartment.

Outside, the sun was still high and bright, a huge, white orb in a flawless sky. The city had thawed; life had busted out full force. The terraces at the cafés were at full capacity; at every table, smiling faces tipped toward the sun. The natives sprawled out on the embankment, letting the sun bake the dampness out of their bones. Across the river, the Paris Plages had finally fulfilled their destiny, with not a speck of sand to spare. People were clustered together in groups of three or more—bedsheets, the urban-dweller's beach blanket, spread out on the sand, end to end.

Stupid me, I'd wasted so much of this day. I comforted myself that there was still more left. Summer days were long in Paris.

I crossed the Pont d'Arcole to the plaza of Hôtel de Ville. A beach volleyball pit had been set up, and a game was on. The crowd had taken sides, lining up around the perimeter. Cops against firemen.

Two teams of dashing public servants in shorts and tight tees jumped around in the sand, leapt in the air. I joined the crowd of spectators, but I found it impossible to choose a side.

On rue des Archives, the bars and cafés were as full as those on Île Saint-Louis. I didn't see any available tables at Léon's restaurant, inside or out, but before I could get worked up over it, a couple vacated a table outside, by the door. Meant to be.

I didn't see Léon straight off, but I wasn't worried. He'd find me. A different waiter came out. I ordered an Aperol spritz. Léon was probably handling the tables inside. No problem. I took out my computer and started to noodle some notes.

Thirty minutes later, no Léon.

Four thirty rolled around. I motioned the waiter over. "Is Léon here?"

"Not today."

What?

I knew he'd said Sunday until five. What had happened? Oh, come on, Paris! *Why do you hate me?* Paris and I had not been in sync since I'd arrived here this trip. Why? It had always been the one place I could count on. Whatever was brewing in my head, or my soul, resolved itself after a stay in Paris. The city always lifted me up, made me stronger, restored my faith in humanity.

Now it was doing the exact opposite.

I'd come here in good faith, because Paris had promised me happiness. I'd walked away from everything for this place. Now it was turning its back on me.

Paris, my fickle lover.

Nothing struck more fear in my heart than the post office, La Poste. Even back in New York, where I could speak the language, I was afraid of the postal workers, who rarely seemed happy to see their customers. La Poste was a treacherous mix: civil workers and a prestigious institution—in a foreign country.

The French Post Office was one of the most important entities in France. More than a mail delivery system, it was also a bank, La Banque Postale, where you could handle all your financial needs: pay bills, change money, apply for credit cards and loans, even buy insurance.

If you needed to send a fax, make photocopies or phone calls, you could also do it at La Poste. It was a center of Parisian daily life, and very hard to avoid if you were spending any amount of time in the country.

I'd avoided it as long as I could, but now I had to send a letter registered mail for my leak case. Once again, that damned leak was responsible for hastening my initiation into real French life. I suppose that was an upside, one might even say a *gift*—if one weren't quaking outside the post office on rue Léon-Frot.

I took a deep breath and walked inside. Just a few patrons. A woman sitting behind a desk looked up as I entered, then looked down again. Self-serve machines lined one wall. Some were blue and yellow, some gray and yellow. What was the difference? I looked over at the woman again. Then at the machines. The woman. The machines.

Nope, not today.

A few days later, I tried the post office on rue Faidherbe. I'd been here once before, with Geoffrey a few years back. Maybe I'd find a friendly face here.

It was packed with customers, several different lines snaking around inside the small space. Just a few self-serve machines, and I still hadn't figured out blue from gray. It wasn't going to happen here, either. Maybe tomorrow I'd come back with reinforcements. I definitely needed reinforcements.

"You're so *timid*. What's wrong with you!" my mother would say to me. When I was about seven or eight, she made me order for myself at Nathan's. Pushed me up to the counter. "Go!" Why was she punishing me? What had I done? How could she be so *cruel*?

She was mystified as to how I'd gotten that way. According to her, I came from a family of bold women. When my grandmother was still a new immigrant in Buffalo, a potato vendor in the market was trying to take advantage of her lack of English. As the story goes, my grandmother stormed off, grabbed a policeman by the arm, and dragged him over to the man trying to rip her off. She got what she needed. It takes guts to stick up for yourself like that, in a strange place where you don't speak the language. I ought to know.

But I am not my grandmother.

I'm my aunt Nicky. Nicoletta was my mother's second-oldest sister. Sweet, gentle Aunt Nicky adopted strays and nursed baby birds. She crocheted our doll clothes and made us funny hats on Christmas Eve from leftover scraps of foil wrapping paper. Though she never had any children of her own, she treated her four nieces like her babies.

Her role in the family was to take care of everyone else—stay at home, cook and clean. Ma said it was her sister "Nig," as they called her, who really raised her, because Gramma was plagued with illness. When Aunt Nicky learned of Ma's death, she lamented, "The baby shouldn't die first." She went to sleep a few days later and never woke up. There was no one left to care for.

With the exception of a brief stint in a factory during World War II, Aunt Nicky never had a life outside the house she grew up in. Even after our grandparents died, she shared that house with her sister, my aunt Helen, both remaining unmarried. She never left the house unless she absolutely had to—a wedding, a luncheon, shopping for the household. After a certain age, when arthritis crippled her, she never left the house at all. My grandmother had willed the property to her, and inside its safe and familiar walls, Nicoletta was master of the universe. Outside? Another story.

I understand my aunt Nicky. I've dreaded any new experience, any disruption to my routine, any situation where I might be held to ridicule because I didn't know what I was doing. I like things mapped out, well planned and rehearsed. I'm the person who walks the little man around in the map program for a virtual dry run so I won't get lost in a new area. Learning how to do essential everyday things in Paris was walking in new territory, without a dry run, and most probably a minefield of doubt and humiliation.

I think I've been this way since that day Ma wept as she walked me to the bus on my first day of school, her tears telling me that something was wrong with my leaving the safety of home, and her.

Or maybe there's still a part of my mind living in that house in

New Jersey, unsure whether today would be a good day or bad, not being able to control the unexpected unhappiness that overtook us suddenly, like a tsunami on a clear day. Overwhelmed by fear of the unknown, by the thought of losing control, I felt small and insignificant.

Hadn't I bought an apartment in Paris, and renovated it from across an ocean? Left a high-paying job to start my life over in a new country? Was I really still that timid little girl, after all I'd accomplished? Afraid of another human being at the *post office?*

Sure, if I screwed up the important daily tasks, bad things *could* happen—such as the letter I was trying to mail not getting to my lawyer. But that letter was never going anywhere as long as I kept carrying it around in my purse.

Okay, tomorrow for sure.

Maybe.

"Paris feels strange. Everything is so hard."

I spilled my guts over tea at the home of an expat friend, also a Lisa, whom I'd known since high school. She'd been living in Paris for the last ten years, married to a Frenchman who calls us *les Deux Lisas*, "the two Lisas." If anyone could understand what this Lisa was going through, it would be the other Lisa.

I told her I was trying hard to stay positive, to find joy along the way. I confessed I felt guilty I was complaining at all—First World problems and all that. I knew how lucky I was, how grateful I should have been. "Maybe I just don't have what it takes." *Maybe I don't deserve this.*

Lisa smiled quietly as I spoke, like someone at peace with herself. "You've just had *huge* change in your life." She said I wasn't giving myself enough credit. "That's a lot to handle. What did you expect?"

I didn't expect to feel like a *failure.*

I was the one who always got straight As. I had to be the best at everything. There were people back home cheering me on, expecting me to succeed, and I was letting them down. "I'm afraid of everything," I confessed. "Like the post office yesterday. And today, I couldn't understand the train conductor, and it gave me an anxiety attack." Was all this just about the leak? "I can't get past the *fear*."

Lisa told me about the time she went to renew her residence card, how the woman at Immigration at the Prefecture de Paris yelled at her about some paper she didn't have. "But I couldn't understand what I needed to do. I just started to cry. Right there. At her window."

Lisa was the bravest person I knew. While I just vacationed in Paris, Lisa left her whole life behind, moved here with no connections, and carved out a life. She inspired me, seemed invincible, someone who just strode out into the world and took life by the balls. "I can't picture you having a meltdown."

"I was building up to it," she said. "Everything was harder than I thought. There was so much I didn't know how to do." She told me she'd had the same fears at the post office, too, in the beginning. "Little things became huge things. And when you don't speak the language, it's *worse*."

Anxiety, she told me, was totally normal. "You're starting over. No one said that would be easy."

Certainly not the way I was doing it. I didn't just walk away from the security of a twenty-year career; I compounded that by leaving the safety of my own country to live in a foreign one. And the one constant I thought I could count on, my little Paris apartment, my home, was no longer an option.

No wonder I felt as if I were in exile. Cut off from everything familiar, how could I not feel lost? "So fear is okay?"

"What's that quote? 'Courage is not the absence of fear'?" Lisa said. "Keep going. It'll get better. I promise." She said she was proud of me, and I should be proud of me, too.

I'd gone way out there, farther than I'd ever been, and it was all uncharted from here. There was no little man I could walk around a map to help me with my life now. This was why the endless days made me anxious, why I had to make schedules. I needed order, something concrete to latch on to in the vast unknown.

I was still being the fixer, still furiously spinning to keep things feeling normal. But normal had changed, and the girl with the broom who swept up chaos couldn't contain it anymore.

Life had gotten too big for small thinking.

I was in a state of expansion, stretching in every direction, so I'd need to get used to feeling uncomfortable, Lisa told me. It wasn't something to fix; it was a marker to be embraced, like fear, telling me I was exactly where I needed to be. But I had to believe I was worthy of a bigger life, and I had little experience in that kind of thinking. Self-worth was yet more uncharted territory. Another trail I'd have to blaze for myself.

That night, I looked up the quote Lisa had mentioned earlier. It was from Ambrose Redmoon: "Courage is not the absence of fear, but rather the judgment that something else is more important than fear."

I'd been inspired in the moment Lisa recalled the fragment of Redmoon's quote, but it didn't take hold. Soldiers have courage, people who fight disease in Africa. I didn't feel courageous. To tell someone fearful to have courage was like telling someone overweight to think thin. It wasn't inspiring; it was bewildering. But seeing the quote in its entirety, I felt the message shake me by the shoulders. *Courage* wasn't the empowering word; it was *judgment*. Redmoon had given me an action plan. Maybe I didn't have courage, but I could make a choice about my life. Right now.

There was something else more important than the fear: Me.

After my mother's death, I chose hope and bought the apartment. Now I was choosing to thrive, and had made the first steps toward a more fulfilling life. I told myself I wouldn't need courage; I would just need to choose to be happy and then do whatever it took to stay that way. I could do that. Right?

Something untied in my gut, and my writer's block finally lifted.

I crossed Pont Saint-Louis from Île Saint-Louis on the way to my beautiful island of exile, like Napoléon on Elba. This was now my everyday route to conduct my extraordinary life—the rolling Seine, the flying buttresses of Notre Dame, my everyday extraordinary view.

On the bridge, an old man with a huge gray beard recited poetry loudly from a book on a music stand. A few paces down, a young man with bushy brown hair was singing Neil Young's "Heart of Gold."

Tourist Paris—a concoction of wonder and grotesquery that both charmed and horrified.

The bells of Notre Dame struck the hour. It was the Feast of the Assumption so they were particularly musical, calling the masses to Mass.

Storm clouds were rolling in again; threatening the one sunny day we'd had in a while. The sun fought for dominance, the Hôtel de Ville bright orange against the stormy gray-blue clouds.

The bells of Notre Dame clanged louder.

In the large bag on my shoulder, supplies from the Monop' on rue de Rivoli: smaller, noncommittal versions of everything I had in my own home in the 11th, a reminder of my circumstance. I still could not settle in, could not rest my soul in this transient place of tourists.

That I was self-evicted from my home, squatting here, still gnawed at the base of my brain, like the leak that still dripped unabated, drawing me away from the beauty around me. But the bells of Notre Dame would not relent. Louder and louder they grew—jubilant, exuberant.

You are in Paris! You are in Paris!

I stopped on the bridge and took a photo of the Seine and the orange Hôtel de Ville, a tourist beside me doing likewise. I drank it in as he did, let it move me as it did him. *Be happy.* There was something to be said about seeing Paris like a tourist, removed from the cares of life. The everyday transmuted to extraordinary. I was starting to forget that wide-eyed wonder, the reason I'd come here in the first place. So, for now, I would stay like this, observing, snapping away. Misty-eyed as I listened to the bells of Notre Dame.

Standing on the bridge suspended over the river, I felt myself in a suspended state, too—my life in Paris not a dream anymore, but not quite real, either. I didn't fight it; I let myself exist in the space between the two, hanging in the air like the vibrations of the bells of Notre Dame after they'd rung their last.

Be happy.

Fourteen

Liberation

Back in the 11th arrondissement—temporarily. I needed more clothes, a few supplies. Fabien met me at the Reuilly–Diderot Métro station, to help carry things back to Île de la Cité. But what I really needed was his emotional support. It had been nearly three weeks since I'd been inside my apartment. What would I find?

The damp could be felt as soon as we entered the lobby. In the ceiling of the hallway, water stains appeared. And that familiar mustiness hung over us, filling my nostrils. I closed my mouth, not wanting to taste its bitterness. Had the mold infected the whole building?

On the next level, we found the ceiling and wall buckled and peeling. More of the same on my floor, but much worse.

This disease was spreading; it was unstoppable. While the owner and the managing agent were playing politics, our house was falling apart. How could this be allowed? Did no one care but me? There were at least forty other apartments in the building. Surely now that the damage was affecting the entire building, someone else would have to care, right? Someone else would have to help me. Wouldn't they?

The front door of my apartment didn't swing open after I

unlocked it. In fact, it wouldn't give way no matter how hard I pushed. Fabien looked at me with big, round eyes. He shook his head. Together we pushed on the door, but it would open only about a foot. We squeezed ourselves inside.

What was happening to my sweet little house? If there was ever a time a girl needed her mother, this was it.

"Putain, le parquet est gonflé!" Fabien declared.

This is how you learn French, when calamity presents specific examples of just how badly you're screwed. *Gonflé* = "swollen."

Fabien bent down and pushed on a floorboard. It gave way easily. "Et moulleux."

Soft.

Then he spewed off a slew of expletives that I could only assume meant the person responsible was less than respectable and should go somewhere unpleasant where they would be made to suffer some form of physical violation. Or maybe that was just what I wanted.

The bubbling now covered three quarters of my wall in the entryway. Large chucks of plaster were peeling away from the wall. New bubbling had sprouted above the front door, and in the bathroom around the light fixture. Was that safe? Water near electricity? I thought of sparks and the ensuing fire consuming my happy place.

My floor was *gonflé* and *moulleux* all the way from the front door to the windows on the other side of the apartment. Repairing all this would surely cost more than the renovation.

This was just three weeks later; what would happen in three months? Six?

"The smell isn't so bad, though." Fabien tossed me a bone. "Not like before. It's better."

Better: *Mieux.*

The smell was the only thing that had improved. Two weeks of airing out seemed to lessen it—but my constricting bronchial tubes told me the mold was as strong as ever.

I shoved some clothes in a large laundry tote—warmer things and some favorite items I'd left behind. I grabbed another bottle of wine, a few more toiletries—pieces of home to carry away with me.

"I'm taking photos of this new damage," I said, whipping out my phone and snapping away—the new bubbling, the ceiling, the door, and all the common areas. "This is bullshit." Tomorrow, a full dossier would be hitting the email inboxes of the board and the managing agent. I would make them care. I would make them help me. Enough of this.

"Get me out of here." Back to the other apartment, to what had somehow become my new haven.

An empty café table in the sun on Île Saint-Louis begged for an occupant. But I was busy; I'd made a list of to-dos to fill my day. My mind was already at the grocery store up the street, so I walked on.

So many times, I'd see a charming café that I'd wanted to have lunch in, but all my friends worked or were away on vacation, and I didn't want to sit alone. So I'd walk away. Hungry.

But today I caught myself. Would it make me happy to sit at that table in the sun?

It was the *only* vacant table in a prime location facing Pont Saint-Louis and the river. Should I sit there? Was it okay? What would I do, just order a drink? Didn't they need the table for other people?

Sit your ass at that table! came a scream in my head. *Be happy.*

It took constant reminding, moment to moment, because happiness wasn't my default emotion. There was always something in the way, some issue, something to question or tweak. Creative director's prerogative perhaps. Or me just being my mother's daughter—conditional happiness based on elusive perfection. It wasn't about the glass being half full or half empty; that wasn't even the point. I would complain about the shape of the glass.

I sat at the table but didn't settle in, couldn't rest at ease in happiness. Suddenly very aware of the people on either side of me, I contracted my body. I told myself I'd stay for only twenty minutes, just enough so I wouldn't regret squandering a chance to sit here. Then I'd give up the table to its rightful owner. Whoever that was. It wasn't me, because I was busy; I had stuff to do.

I ordered a cool drink. See? Here I was, sitting at the table. Good, right? This was what was known as making oneself happy, and I was doing it.

Who do you think you are?

No, I deserved this. I was going to stay right here. Maybe even have two drinks, because that would make me happy—no matter how awkward "happy" felt.

Okay, so this is nice. Wonder when the waitress is bringing that drink. The sky is gorgeous; I really should be taking photos of this stuff. No, come on, stay in the moment . . . Oh good, the drink is here!

The chatter was back. The fill-my-head banter so I wouldn't feel lonely—or maybe it was so I wouldn't feel, period.

I shut down the chatter and sat sipping, looking out at the tourists on the bridge.

Sorry. Sorry. So sorry.

Under the chatter, there it was: shame and guilt. But whom was I apologizing to?

"You're going to Paris *again?*"

This was something I'd hear every time I told my mother I was leaving for my other city.

"Yeah, Ma. I go twice a year. Every year."

"But you just went! What if something happens to me? It's so far away."

If I had been feeling excited about my vacation, I wasn't anymore. Instead, I was remembering my fear of flying, all the work I had to finish before I left, those scary unknowns that lay ahead.

Fragile again.

I dreaded this phone call; it was always the same. She could never just say, "Oh, great! Have fun. Bring me something nice." The point was I was going off and having fun on my own, having something that was mine alone.

"Why do you always have to go to Paris? Are you ever going to Italy again?"

So now I was being made to feel guilty for neglecting my people? "Sure, Ma. I'll go to Italy with you. Let's plan it."

"Oh, you never have time. You're always running off to Paris."

Why did I think I could come away unscathed from this call? I was dealing with the master of manipulation. I was spinning again.

It took courage for me to get on a plane and fly across an ocean. I dreaded travel, never liked leaving the safety of home. Ma knew that because she was the same. What I needed was encouragement, reassurance that all would be well. But her insecurity and fears wouldn't permit that. Instead, I got my own fears handed to me on a plate. With a big side dish of guilt.

Who do you think you are?

My trip to Paris would be tainted. I would no longer feel free to enjoy myself without thinking of Ma worrying about me, alone at home missing out on the fun. I was a terrible, selfish daughter running off to Paris twice a year. Leaving her.

My grandmother did the same to my mother. Especially anytime Ma wanted to go out with her friends, do something on her own. What did she mean running off on a Sunday to go to the beach? After her mother had made a big meal? Did she think her friends were more important than family?

After Gramma died, her sisters took over, berating Ma for wanting to see her friends when we were visiting Buffalo for such a short time. How could we not spend all the time with them? "These are my *childhood* friends," Ma would argue. She'd turn herself inside out to schedule the visits, using the least amount of time. Sometimes we'd see two families in one day. Her stress was palpable. She'd work so hard to please her family, but it never seemed enough. I often had the sense that if Ma could have spent the entire trip with her friends, she would have.

Ah, family.

Ma was the youngest of four daughters, and there were eight years between her and the second youngest. Ma's oldest sister, Mary, was a teenager in the late 1920s. In those days, she still had to lie about her last name, becoming Mary Smith in order to get work, because no one would hire an Italian at a fine shop. Ma was a teenager fifteen years later, and by then a huge cultural shift had happened in the country. My mother was an alien to her family, fully embodying the exuberance and optimism of the Big Band era, the rebellious one who somehow was never really seen as anything else, even years later.

When I was a child, I'd watch how often they'd dig at her—her mother, her sisters. "That's a strange-looking haircut," they said of her very trendy shag. Or "Always slacks. Do you ever wear a skirt? Are you *liberated* now?" If she had a new idea to offer, it was "Is that how they do things in *New Jersey*?" They'd wear down her spirit over the course of the trip. She was always explaining herself, her ideas, her lifestyle. *Poor Ma*, I'd think. She was stylish and perfect. What was their problem?

Even years later, when Ma was in her late fifties, her family could still push every button. On a visit one summer, Ma had an anxiety attack that nearly sent her to the hospital. "I'm never coming here again," she swore to my father. "Never again!" And she didn't for many years, until her sister Mary died. Her family would visit us in New Jersey, but no way was she setting foot on their turf again.

"The best thing I ever did was move away," she confessed to me after that horrific anxiety-ridden visit. When we first moved to New Jersey she was miserable without her family, but years later she realized it had been good for her to get some distance.

I didn't understand why she let her family get to her, but here I was, well into adulthood, squirming inside from one phone call with my mother.

Though Ma suffered from the constant belittling her family gave her, when her daughters tried to make their own lives, she could only respond to us the way her family had to her—with guilt and manipulation.

She couldn't help herself; it was too much a part of her psyche to change.

But if it was all her issue and not mine, why did I feel it was wrong of me to want something just for me? To indulge myself and have fun?

I ordered another drink at my sunny café table.

As I sat sipping, a green army jeep pulled up in front of the café. Inside, two men and a woman dressed in military khakis—but not French uniforms, vintage American. And the jeep was a relic, too, definitely from World War II. There'd been a parade earlier in the day, part of a series of events celebrating the seventieth anniversary of the city's liberation from Nazi occupation. I'd forgotten to go. I took a photo of the jeep with my phone and told myself it was almost the same thing.

But did I forget to go to the parade, or was I so wrapped up in being miserable that I didn't want to change that? Did I like missing out? Was deprivation my natural resting state?

My parents were born in the Depression, and their parents were poor immigrants. This was my legacy. It was always about being grateful with the scraps and not complaining. It explains why I'd put up with less in everything—from staying at a table next to a smoker to not asking for a raise at work.

In our family, especially among the older generation, anyone who attempted to indulge oneself received a shaming. You were being "wasteful" and "irresponsible." The implied message: *How could you be splurging when I'm going without?*

Did I see taking care of myself as a shameful indulgence? How many times had I tolerated an unhealthy situation, or suffered through discomfort? Yet gritting your teeth and sticking it out makes you brave, doesn't it? Isn't it noble to suffer?

Or had I just been guilted into it?

Go without. Do with less. Save it for others. This was how we were raised, and how my mother had been raised. When we emptied our childhood home, we found brand-new 300-thread-count linens still in the original packaging from the 1980s. Plush towels, also new. They had been saved "for good," meaning guests— or the queen. Who knows? The point was they were too good for Ma to use. Spend money on them? Sure. But use them? Not "good" enough. So there they sat for years. Doing nobody any good.

Ma went through her whole life without ever treating herself to the simple luxury of a soft, thick towel after a bath. Did she think herself so unworthy of the good stuff in life?

Did I?

I wondered if it would be a kind of betrayal to indulge myself when Ma never did. Or was she in heaven telling me to go for it? *Take care of yourself, baby girl.*

I sipped hard on my drink. A horrible thought popped into my head. Did I think it was wrong to have fun while Ma was dead?

Why do you have to go away to Paris and leave me? It's so far away.

Was deprivation my penance?

Or maybe I was just using Ma as an excuse, as always, not to get out there and really live my life.

The jeep moved on. The table to my right had a new inhabitant, a woman by herself, like me. When the waitress came by, she looked at my drink, pointed. Maybe she thought, *I'm going to sit at that table and be like that woman.* I might have inspired her, but she had no idea of the mess going on inside my head.

Another cloudy day in Paris. I buried my manicured toes in the sand, pulled my scarf tighter around my shoulders. A long barge of shipping containers eased under Pont Notre-Dame on its way upriver.

My friend Adrian and I sat on blue-and-white canvas lounges under a big umbrella, even though there wasn't a ray of sun to be had, and sipped rosé from plastic cups. Wedged between our chairs, a straw tote packed with a container of couscous, a can of almonds, and some crudité with taramasalata, or salmon roe dip.

Sixty-five degrees, but damn it! We would have our picnic on the Paris Plages. Our tenacity was echoed by our fellow picnickers. Parisians' spirits can't be squelched by a little rain, not in a city where rainy days outnumber sunny ones. Still, this summer was one of the coldest they'd had in years. The leaves on the chestnut trees were already starting to turn.

A red fishing boat with a tin roof chugged by. Our stack of napkins blew away in a gust of wind. It was bitter, but I refused to be. I pretended it was Labor Day in the Hamptons.

"This is why people leave the city in August," Adrian said. She herself had just returned from Nice. Dressed in white cotton to show off her tan, she was the summeriest thing on this beach.

Most Parisians had deserted the city for beaches warmer than this one by the Seine. One by one, I had watched shops and restaurants close down for les congés, as they called it, posting signs of their planned absence: WE INFORM OUR AMIABLE CLIENTELE THAT WE WILL BE CLOSED FOR VACATION FROM 1 AUGUST TO 8 SEPTEMBER INCLUDED.

Me, I used to feel guilty about taking time off, time that was owed me. At my old job, we all apologized for taking a few days away, even though we'd worked hard for them. So what was wrong with us, huh?

Only in France would it be okay to halt commerce for nearly six weeks. Then again, who would they be staying open for? You were expected to skedaddle yourself. Your favorite café, the local bread or cheese shop—all closed down. Even the patter of your neighbor's footfall vanished. So what were you still doing here? *Allez! Hop! Hop!*

The dead of August was less noticeable here in the touristy center of town, but you could tell by who stayed open and who did not which businesses catered to the tourist trade and which were local favorites. I made a note of that so, in September, I'd have a whole new list of must-try local restaurants.

We polished off the wine as a Batobus motored past with its cargo of tourists, who waved at us. An empty flat-bottom barge inched along in the other direction on the way to being filled again.

Looking out at the Seine for a long time, all I could see were the boats. I never realized how constant the river traffic was, a watery universe unto itself. At first, it was the movement of the boats I noticed, calming me as they drifted by. But an hour in, I started to notice the boats themselves, each different, each with its own purpose. They came to life, their unique personalities contributing to the story of the city, like the Parisians themselves.

A speedboat whipped past, POLICE written on its side. It was, of course, the sexiest of all the boats.

"Shall we?" said Adrian, popping the lids back on the food containers.

I brushed the sand off my feet. "Well, we can say we've done it." I stuffed my chilly toes back into my Converse Low Tops.

"I'm glad we did," Adrian said. "Aren't you?"

I nodded. Even gladder to have someone to share it with, to wipe the gloom away. I was dreading that we'd be parting in the next minute, so much of the day left to be alone with my thoughts.

"Do you want to see the Libération exhibit at Hôtel de Ville?" she asked.

"Sure. Sounds great." *Grateful* was more like it. An invitation in the nick of time.

The exhibit in the city hall building was another part of the Libération of Paris celebration. Photographs and ephemera from the era were hung around a darkened gallery space two stories high. The crowd moved soberly around the room, paying respects to the relics, Charles de Gaulle's voice filling the hall, playing on a loop from a film projected on a massive screen: "Paris, outraged. Paris, broken. Paris, martyred. But Paris, liberated. Liberated by itself. Liberated by its people."

Ma would have loved this.

The photos were the most riveting, scenes of the struggle for freedom frozen in graphic detail: Parisians sacrificing their beautiful city to transform it into a battleground, digging up their paving stones to build makeshift barricades, exploding mortar shells around their own monuments. I leaned in close and scrutinized the images, trying to put myself in the scene, but in the end, I was grateful for the black-and-white photos, and time, making it history.

We'd always been taught the Americans just rolled in and sent the Nazis running with their hands and white flags in the air—one grand, sweeping gesture that brought freedom overnight. But the fight for liberation was slow, insidious; it was all day, every day. And Parisians were willing to create chaos in their world to achieve it.

Here I was complaining about how cold it was, that I had to move to a vacation rental, when seventy Augusts ago, Parisians were dying for their freedom. I'd just gotten a big dose of perspective.

On the way back to my temporary lodging, I walked through the former battlegrounds for liberation, now reclaimed by peace, gloriously restored. A visitor to the city would never know anything had happened, but the scars were still there, and now I could see them: bullet holes in the façade of Hôtel-Dieu de Paris; gashes from mortar shells in the Conciergerie, jagged as the day they were made, decades of soot clinging to the rough edges of the gaping wounds.

They'd never patched these up, never smoothed them over. Perhaps to remember that when you cut yourself free from what's holding you back, it's not without violence and pain.

Tourists walked around Île Saint-Louis enraptured, gawking at the Seine and the ancient buildings lining it. On rue Jean-du-Bellay, they scooted into the café tables, wriggling in their seats, unable to contain the excitement twitching in their muscles. They queued twenty deep at ten o'clock in the morning for ice cream at Berthillon, their eyes wide as they took their first taste.

Paris made them children with full hearts and dreamy heads.

Before today, they'd been a nuisance, grotesque and consumerist. A mockery of everything I was trying to accomplish in Paris, forcing me to live among them like a tourist myself. Surrounded by happy tourists, always in pairs or family groups, I'd been feeling even more alone. They reminded me of home and how far I was from everything familiar. It was easy to ridicule them, be annoyed by them, but really I wanted to be having fun like them—with them.

Something inside me gave way: my need to belong, to feel safe, cleaved me to the tourists. They were me, trying to experience their Paris dream, too. Who was I to resent them?

No longer evading their clusters, stomping past their obtrusiveness, annoyed, I walked among them, watching their faces as they experienced the city for the first time, as I had once done twenty years before. The city became enchanting again. Their enjoyment became mine.

I'd been hoarding Paris, holding on to it too tightly, as if I were afraid it wasn't really mine, that I was a pretender. I'd forgotten other people had a claim on Paris, too—and yes, sometimes that placed them in my way, but that's what happens when you become part of the world: other people are there.

Paris was to be shared, and so was my Paris experience. As I started to open myself up, people began to engage me in conversation. "You live here, and you're American?" they'd say. "Do you know any good places to eat around here?"

Did I know any good places? I had years of information stowed in my head; I overflowed with it: the best restaurants in the Latin Quarter that wouldn't rip them off, my favorite places to picnic on the Seine, which city bus lines had the best views—"Way cheaper than those commercial tour buses."

Why not share what I knew? What was I saving it for?

Or was it me I was saving? Waiting for when I felt ready and perfect enough before I opened up to the world? Had I made myself the lonely outsider—not just here in Paris, but in life?

Helping the tourists got me out of my own head and into the world. And the more people I helped, the happier I became. *This shop has the cutest gifts, and the owner won't hawk you . . . That street is hard to find; let me take you there.* I knew what it was to be lost and uneasy in a foreign place. If I could change a look of stress into a smile of relief, why not? It's what I did best, right? Fixing things? Maybe it was time to use that power for good, huh? The more I shared what I knew about the city, the more I belonged to it. Paris didn't feel strange anymore.

By freeing myself of the expectations of what was supposed to happen to me in Paris, I was allowing myself to enjoy the experiences that were actually happening.

It hadn't been the tourists' fault I wasn't enjoying Paris the way I'd wanted. Or the leak's fault. Or the weather's. I'd set myself up for failure before I even came here.

In the past, I'd just allow Paris to serve up whatever it would, which is why it felt so effortless, but this time I'd brought a bundle of expectations with me, because after so much change, I needed a road map, a security blanket. Doing that changed my relationship with the city. There was no way Paris would ever measure

up, because my need for everything to be perfect was so unfor-
giving.

As always, I was trying to sweep the unpleasant things into
compartments so I wouldn't have to feel their effects, and could
carry on. The harder I fought against my emotions, the more fragile I became—and the more fragile, the greater my need to control
my environment. Instead of feeling safe, I just made myself anxious, angry, and depressed. In Paris.

I'd been in crisis mode, that child again in a home where things
could be turned on end without notice. Maybe I'd never been out
of crisis mode; maybe this was the story I was writing for myself
over and over until somehow there'd be a different ending.

During those three months my sister and I spent emptying our
childhood home, I coped by being ultraorganized and working
hard, packing up and labeling dozens of boxes a day. Pack it up,
tape it shut, stow it away. Yeah, I'm a pro at that. That's always how
I dealt with pain.

But day by day, I was letting go and letting things happen, freeing myself. I could sense an unclenching inside, a surrender to
what I was really feeling: I was in mourning—for my old job, for
my old life, for Ma. I had been hanging on to everything around
me, trying to hang on to something that was already gone, but if
I let go, I'd have to experience the loss. And I was tired of experi-
encing loss. I'd come to Paris to be happy.

But I only started to be happy when I opened up and let myself
feel my pain.

Trying to cordon off negative emotions, shutting down a part
of myself—how could I expect to be happy? It was another
form of deprivation. Life had to be experienced in full, or you
missed out. You can't guard against the bad like Ma had done
with her purse full of remedies. Or deny it, as I had done. All you
can do is let go and let it happen.

Here I'd been running myself ragged trying to get all the bad
stuff out of the way so I could be in this mystical Zen place of

perfect bliss where I'd be able to begin my life in Paris and write. Meanwhile, the bad stuff I was trying to push aside, work through, and fix *was* my life in Paris. It was time to stop waiting to live, and to just live. To liberate myself from perfection and put myself out there—flaws, pain, and all.

PART 4

. . . .

Coming Home

· Fifteen ·

The Homecoming

I'd finally taken my toiletries out of the plastic bag where I'd been keeping them, and put them in the medicine cabinet of my temporary apartment. All my belongings had a place now. The apartment had been accommodating, designed with little creature comforts and well-conceived storage, such as the stackable plastic baskets I'd found in the closet, perfect for tucking things away, organizing loose items in the shower, and keeping food-stuffs in the kitchen. This temporary home helped me to feel contained and comforted when I needed it. Maybe I'd been a mess inside, but the apartment was not. I enjoyed dusting and primping the little gem, having finally embraced it as home.

It had been a halcyon escape from city mayhem. At night, the bedroom was dark and quiet, especially compared to my own place in the 11th, which was directly across from a streetlamp that shone like the sun all night long, flooding my apartment with light. I had to wear an eye mask like Audrey Hepburn in *Breakfast at Tiffany's*, but without any of the glamour. My street, as small as it was, was inordinately noisy: students yammering all day at top volume, their class bell ringing every forty minutes. At night, we had a steady stream of drunken revelers from nearby bars.

Yet, here on Île de la Cité, I'd enjoyed so many restful nights, I almost felt a little guilty about it. Did I deserve such luxury?

I'd settled into a routine in the neighborhood, found my writing spot: a café on rue de Rivoli where they let me sit all day and work. I'd show up around eleven in the morning, order a coffee, and write a bit, then pause for lunch and write until about five in the afternoon, when, invariably, one of my friends would pop by for an *apéro* before dinner. I had a favorite table, ordered one of the same three things: eggs Benedict, chicken paillard, or, if I was hungover, the burger. Routine felt like home.

In spite of the August vacations, this area was still lively, and it kept me feeling a part of a community. I realized what a blessing that had been; my locals-only neighborhood would have been deserted and lonely. I was grateful now for this apartment. It had been a gift. When else would I have had the chance to live in this district?

No matter what I was doing, even mundane errands, I got to do it surrounded by views of the river lined by some of the most beautiful buildings in Paris, with plaques that reminded me how ancient they were:

THE HOUSE OF PHILIPPE DE CHAMPAIGNE, PAINTER AND CHAMBER VALET OF THE QUEEN MOTHER. 1643.

I'd always wondered how my Roman friend felt when she'd pass by the Coliseum each day on her way to the market. Now I knew.

The apartment's central location spoiled me. In one minute, I could cross the river into the Right Bank and be in the Marais; cross to the Left Bank: the Latin Quarter. I'd alternate my grocery shopping between the Monoprix near the Sorbonne, among the students, and the smaller Monop' on rue de Rivoli, with the young, rich professionals—just because I could.

You could walk around the perimeter of Île Saint-Louis in fifteen minutes, twenty if you dawdled. And I did, often, always discovering something new. Such a small patch of earth, but there'd often be a house, shop, or lane I hadn't seen before—like a recurring dream I'd have where I'd open a door in my apartment and discover a whole new suite of rooms I never knew existed. I was like that dream, opening up and expanding in ways I didn't think possible. It had been an emotional roller coaster with extreme highs and plummeting lows, but I was finally starting to enjoy the ride.

Geoffrey and Christophe had returned from their vacation in Lyon, so the gang was together again, and they loved the apartment. "You should move here!" they kept saying. I had been worried that living in the center of town would have put me too far from my friends, but the 4th arrondissement was a favorite hangout, and friends came often, stayed long. I'm sure my neighbors facing the courtyard were driven mad by Geoffrey's laugh. We'd celebrated his birthday in the apartment, an intimate group of seven people. It was humble—nothing like the themed extravaganzas Geoffrey would normally have thrown—but he loved it because he loved being in my little apartment on Île de la Cité. I loved it, too.

Too bad it was time to leave.

New tenants were moving in September 1, and I'd spent all morning scrubbing the place, changing the sheets, vacuuming, cleaning out the refrigerator—removing any traces of my having been there. That had been part of the deal. Over the weeks, I'd accumulated clothes and supplies; I'd even bought a travel blow dryer and a fan at BHV. Now it all had to be transported back.

I was supposed to have been gone hours ago. A friend, Tammy, was going to meet me near my apartment in the 11th, and we'd have lunch at my local café near Place Léon-Blum. But I was still all over the place—bags half packed, still trying to clean up and get everything in order. I couldn't focus, and I was filled with dread and anxiety. Again.

I didn't want to go.

Tammy ended up coming to help me pack. Five large tote bags, two plastic bags of groceries, a small suitcase, and a BHV shopping bag containing the fan I'd bought. I called a taxi to get it all across town.

The bells of Notre Dame rang two o'clock.

"I'm going to miss that," I said, looking out at the courtyard. The ivy clinging to its walls was turning red, a sign summer was coming to an end. I shut the window for the last time, drew the curtains.

My throat tightened with emotion. This was why I couldn't get my things packed up, why I was spinning. Yet again, I was holding on. How long I'd fought being here, and now that I was leaving, I wanted to stay.

I could only laugh at myself.

Tammy and I waited outside for the taxi. Clouds hung over us, but it wasn't cold. A few motocops milled about in front of their station. "I'm going to miss them, too," I joked.

The monumental pile of belongings on the sidewalk reminded me of the day when I first arrived, lugging my possessions on the Métro. Why did I make it so hard on myself then? I was already in pain, having to leave a home being damaged by a leak I couldn't control. Did I need to make it worse? Was I punishing myself?

Self-nurturing was still as foreign to me as it was to Ma. And in times of crisis, I usually defaulted to my eight-year-old self. Fix it, get it done. Pain? What pain? Don't mind me, I'm fine.

Maybe a part of me wanted to wallow in misery because somehow I thought what had happened to my apartment was what I deserved. My comeuppance for willfully throwing away a secure job. Not since my grandparents left Europe for a better life in America had anyone in my family taken such a leap of faith, leaving the safe and familiar for the hope of more. The next generation had been encouraged to settle in, get an education, build wealth. If my parents had been alive, they might have steered me away from the risks. Had I felt ashamed that I went against their advice, guilty because I dared to want more for myself?

Who do you think you are?

It didn't matter now. Whatever the reasons, that woman was no more. Four weeks later, I was now the type of person who called for a taxi when she needed it. Asking for help didn't mean I was flawed, it meant I liked myself enough to take care of myself.

The taxi pulled up a few minutes later. Time to go. I took a last, lingering look at my haven from my troubles.

The driver's door flung open. A man jumped out and bowed with a broad sweep of his arm. "Mesdames! Bonjooooooour!" he called out.

Whoa. So much for being allowed to steep in my melancholy.

"I invite you lovely ladies into my taxi!" He opened the door. Another bow. Another wave of his arm. "I will get the bags! That's my great pleasure!" *Mon grand plaisir.*

Tammy and I climbed into the van, chuckling. Clearly, we'd been sent a very special cab for my moving day, because normal Parisian taxi drivers were nothing like this.

"Wow!" the man said as he hopped into the driver's seat, slamming his door. "That's a lot of stuff you have! Are you coming or going?"

I told him I was moving apartments.

"Ah, new home! That's wonderful!"

Old home, I thought.

He sang out my address. "Oui? C'est ça?"

"Oui, monsieur!" I started to get into the game. "Correct!"

"Okay! Let's go to your new home!"

He pulled away from the apartment, but I was too busy laughing to wave good-bye.

"You like music?" our driver asked as we turned the corner toward the bridge en route to the Right Bank.

Of course we did, we assured him.

"Bon! Reggae?"

We loved reggae. Who didn't love reggae?

"Okay!" he said, hitting a button on his dashboard. Before I could remember that I had been uneasy and anxious a few minutes before, Bob Marley told me, "Don't worry about a thing, cuz every little thing is gonna be all right."

Come on. Really? Someone really wanted me to get the message.

The driver spied us in his rearview mirror. "You like it?"

"Sure! Bob Marley!" I said, bobbing along.

"Great!" He hit a switch and the music boomed out of the car, as if from external speakers.

Wait a minute—*were* there external speakers?

Peeking around the front passenger seat, I discovered a full karaoke setup, rigged to some crazy speaker system. Our driver grabbed the microphone and started singing, his voice ringing out into the neighborhood, drawing attention from people crossing Pont d'Arcole.

Our party van boom-boomed as we drove along the river and toward the 11th arrondissement. "I give you the best ride, ladies!" our driver shouted over the music. "Oui?"

"Oui, monsieur!" By then I was convulsing with laughter, tears streaming down my cheeks—the good kind of tears.

Don't worry about a thing, cuz every little thing is gonna be all right.

Back in my own apartment. Water still leaked, mold continued to grow—but armed with prescriptions from my doctor, I could endure staying here for my final few days in Paris.

And it felt good to be home again.

While I was unpacking my bags, my phone buzzed against the table, delivering a text message.

"Welcome back! Happy hour?"

My neighbor Andrea was finally free for our favorite activity: *le Happy Hour* was a concept catching on in Paris, especially in gentrifying neighborhoods such as ours, where all things Brooklyn were de rigueur. We had our favorite café for *le Happy Hour*, and I hadn't been there in a month.

What better way to celebrate my homecoming than with a half-priced beverage?

Walking in the streets of my neighborhood again, it felt like I'd never been away, a wrinkle in time having brought that faraway day when I left, and this one, together. Gone were the cobbled streets and centuries-old churches of my postcard-perfect island. I was back in the real world: vital working-class Paris, tattered but homey.

You could keep your postcard Paris. Nothing was better than the real one.

We snagged a table outside our café. The waitress greeted us with a huge smile, her eyes registering recognition when she saw me. "Where have you been?" she asked. "Vacation?"

She actually looked happy to see me. When I was staying in the center of the city, I went to the same café every day for weeks. No one ever said, "Nice to see you again," or "Welcome back." They weren't rude, but they weren't friendly, either. Working in a café frequented by transients and tourists, it's probably not worth getting personal. Why get attached when you may never see that customer again? But if you live there, how can you ever feel a belonging if everyone is standoffish?

"You ladies having the rosé?" our waitress asked. "Happy Hour?"

"You sure know us," I said.

"Of course!" She popped back inside to get our drinks.

A man who I'd seen here once or twice nodded hello to us as he entered the café. The owner greeted him. The waitress hailed someone passing by, chatted with him for a few minutes, shared a laugh. They kissed each other on both cheeks before he continued on his way, baguette under his arm, heading home for dinner.

How friendly and easy this neighborhood was. I'd forgotten. Or maybe I didn't realize just how friendly it was until I'd lived somewhere that wasn't a tight-knit village like this. We weren't

strangers; we were neighbors bonded by our district. Unpreten-
tious, warm, and genuine—this was home.

It was good to be back.

They call it *la rentrée*, "the reentry"—when everyone comes
back from the August vacations to ready the kiddies for school.
The city wakes up again: shops reopen, the Métro cars fill up.
Our neighborhood buzzed with a resurgence of energy as we re-
united with one another, and our own lives. This was my *rentrée*,
too—I was renewed and ready for whatever was coming.

Sixteen

The Pilgrimage

Gare de Lyon, the Lyon train station, sits near the Seine in the 12th arrondissement. When I came to Paris as a high school student, our raggedy old hotel was just up the street. It could still be found all these years later, but had been completely renovated. A high-end furnishings store, Roche Bobois, had moved in next door; a gallery and shopping district created one block away on Avenue Daumesnil. My, how the neighborhood had changed.

I was on my way to Burgundy for two days to celebrate Christophe's birthday. He and Geoffrey were throwing the bash at the three-hundred-year-old ancestral home of Geoffrey's family, where his parents still lived. I knew his parents well, and had been invited for the week, but since I'd just started to settle back into my apartment, and was leaving the week after for New York, I only wanted to stay the weekend.

The day before my departure, Geoffrey had taken me to the station for a dry run, which he'd insisted on. "I just want to be sure you're okay, my Liza."

It didn't seem like a big deal to take a train. You go to the station, buy the ticket, go to the platform, get on the train, sit for two and a half hours—*et voilà!*—you're there. But apparently, there was a quirk in this particular line I had to be extra careful about.

"The train splits, and half goes one way and the other half goes another way."

I needed to be very sure I was in the correct half of the train, or I'd end up in a totally different part of France.

Uh . . . okay. "How do I know which half?"

"On the side of the train it has to say, 'Avallon,'" he explained. "Aaavaaallon."

To make sure I got it right, he took me to Gare de Lyon to buy the ticket and show me the lay of the land. But the more he stressed what I needed to do, the more it made me think I should have been more concerned about this journey than I was.

The morning of my trip he texted me: "You okay?"

Yeah, should I not be okay?

Then again: "You take Avallon train to Vézelay Sermizelles."

Yup, got it already. "Thanks, sweetie," I texted back.

Then he called. "Are you okay, my Liza? You are on the train?"

"No, sweetie. It's eight thirty. My train is at ten thirty."

"Oh! I thought it was now. I was worried I didn't get your text. So you remember Avallon? Vézelay Sermizelles? Okay?"

How could I forget? "Yes. I'm fine. I arrive at one o'clock."

"Okay. Text me when you are on the train so I will not worry."

I had woken up feeling strong, but now I was stressed. It was nice to have someone worry about me, but now I was also worried about me. Was this more complicated than I thought?

I arrived at the station a full hour before my train, to be sure I had time to find everything. Gare de Lyon has three halls, and Geoffrey had told me they would announce which hall one hour before departure, and the track, or *voie*, just minutes before. He'd walked me to each hall, so I knew just where to find them.

The display showed my train—destination: Avallon—was slated for Hall One. I rode the escalator up from the lower-level shopping concourse to what turned out to be the main hall of the original station from the early 1900s, with a soaring glass atrium supported by steel trusses. People buzzed around, even on a weekend, or sat reading their paper while they sipped espressos at the cafés near the platforms. On the level above, the venerable Le Train Bleu offered more luxury surroundings for coffee sipping, if I were so inclined. I climbed the stairs to peer through the glass doors at the serpentine Art Nouveau molding and gilt ceiling: old Paris. The Parisians had preserved it, keeping it constant. You could stay connected to the past in this city, which is probably why I loved it, and no one here would give me a hard time about my attachment to nostalgia.

From the higher vantage point, where the restaurant was located, the entire station was visible. Sun filtered through the dust-covered glass ceiling, creating soft rays of light over the hall. This was a station like every station ever shown in films set in Europe.

Whatever residual worries I had were trumped by the thrill.

Busy taking photos of the station, I nearly missed my track announcement: *voie* E. The time of reckoning had come. Geoffrey's instructions ran in my head—*Avallon! Avallon! Avallon!* But when I got to the track, the display showed all the stations with a clear graphic, including the split. Under "Avallon," a key piece of information: *Avant du Train.* Front of the train for Avallon.

Well, that was easy. But just to be sure, I got in one of the first three cars. To be doubly—no, triply—sure, I asked three different people, "Avallon?" and was validated three different times—a trinity of yeses. What more would a Catholic girl need?

I texted Geoffrey: "On the train."

We pulled out of the city, traveling through the bleak suburbs, but before long, they gave way to rolling hills, plots of farmland carved by plows, divided by rows of trees. The farther south we traveled, the more clouds we shed, as if unloading the gloom of the city station by station, until at Vézelay-Sermizelles only sun remained, bright and warm.

Geoffrey met me on the platform at Vézelay-Sermizelles. He was just on the other side of the train doors as they opened. I fell out of the train and into his embrace.

"Welcome in Burgundy, my Liza!"

Geoffrey's father was also there to greet me, and drive us to their little village of two hundred people, a short ride through winding roads and more rolling hills.

"We are arrived!" Geoffrey announced as we pulled up to a small enclave of stone buildings behind a gated wall.

"Which house is yours?" I asked.

"All of them. You'll see."

All of them?

The gate opened and we pulled into the complex, the gravel driveway crunching under the tires. A grand two-story white stone house dominated the complex; across from it, a smaller house with an arched doorway and a pitched roof. A grapevine grew on its façade, heavy with red grapes. I thought of my grandmother's house, of the vines my grandfather had brought from Italy and planted in their eight-foot-square yard. They were dormant for years, but they'd exploded full with fruit, like these vines in Burgundy, just before we put the house up for sale—a last hurrah for the heart-broken family about to say good-bye to the little house on Swan Street that had been in our family for eighty-five years.

Nestled beside the main house: a row of three interconnected one-story cottages. On one of them, tacked onto its whitewashed wooden door, a sign in English: COME IN. WE'RE OPEN.

"That's Papa," Geoffrey said, thumbing at the sign. Just one of many quirks on the property, apparently, born of the impish mind of Geoffrey's father, a painter and photographer.

Each of the eight buildings in the complex faced a long yard populated by shade trees, fruit trees, and a graceful weeping willow. On the hill above, just on the other side of their stone wall, a small twelfth-century church with a steeple like a needle looked out over all.

Though this was my first time here, it felt familiar. Was it the grapes, the garden? Or was it simply that taking the train from the city to a home in the country was something I did often over the years, when I'd visit Ma?

She'd always wave good-bye to me from her car as my train pulled out of the station. Not just any run-of-the-mill wave, not Ma. She'd stick her arm way out of the window and wave broadly, regally, with a cupped hand. Sometimes, to spice it up, she'd make a jerking side-to-side motion, like a windshield wiper. I'd stand up at my seat to catch that wave, chuckling and waving back. She'd keep it up until the train was fully out of the station. I'd keep waving until she was out of sight, but it wouldn't have surprised me to learn that Ma kept waving long after, in case I could still see her.

After she became ill, I took a taxi to the station instead, but Ma still gave me her patented queen wave from her front door.

Coming home to Geoffrey's family, I felt the same sense of security. Here I could let my guard down, relax. Let go. That's what home is about.

Christophe was sitting at a table under the trees with Geoffrey's mother and cousins, enjoying an apéritif before lunch. They waved as I approached, but before I could say my hellos, Geoffrey grabbed my hand and whipped me away.

"Come, Liza!" he said, taking my bag from me. "I wanna show you the big house. And we gave you the best room."

The "big house" was where the grandmother had lived, where we'd be staying. Geoffrey explained that his parents lived in the small house, which was originally the kitchen for the château, and still had the large stone hearth where the cooking had been done years ago.

The long entryway of the big house had the original tile floor: a lattice pattern of brown and blue-gray bordered in a Greek key design. The walls were lined with mahogany wainscoting and a screaming floral wallpaper: stylized vines and roses as big as my head, all in shades of browns, rust, and gold. Like something from the 1970s, but the patina told me it was probably one hundred years older, when this décor was the height of fashion. Deeply faded, it had put its most garish years behind it. Instead, it gave the hall kitschy chic.

"This is my ancestor." Geoffrey pointed to a portrait of a woman set in a fat gilt frame. Her glossy brown hair was parted in the middle, a cluster of chin-length banana curls framing each side of her pretty, pale face. She sat serene in a black dress with a white ruffled front panel and Peter Pan collar of transparent lace. Her hair and dress dated the portrait from the 1850s, but her eyes were still very much in the present, living on in Geoffrey's, which were identical in every aspect except for the color. Hers: clear blue-gray; his: deep brown. Like the floor tiles we were standing on.

I envied Geoffrey his uninterrupted link with his past. My family had left everything behind in Italy to immigrate to the States. I'm not even sure where the family home is or if it even still stands. The oldest portrait we have of a family member is a large hand-tinted photograph of my great-grandmother from about 1916, framed in heavy oak. It used to hang over the sofa in the front parlor of Gramma's house, but before I was born. I didn't grow up looking at her, so I have no attachment to the portrait. My history began with my grandmother. Geoffrey's family could trace theirs all the way back to the twelfth century. I wondered if that made a person feel immortal.

Geoffrey showed me around the suite of rooms on the ground floor—the kitchen, where we would have breakfast; and a small chamber beside it with its own tile floor, much more colorful than that in the front hall. "This was the children's dining room," Geoffrey said. I tried to picture him as a child with his siblings sitting around a tiny table having their tiny meals. The room was empty now, except for the fireplace and a chest of drawers, but still cheerful, as though their childhood energy had embedded itself in the walls.

There were two large rooms off the main hall. One, which faced the front of the house, was a comfortable sitting room with a floor of octagonal terra cotta tiles called *tomettes*. A large fireplace, newly restored, was the focal point. More crazy floral wallpaper covered the walls. This must have been all the rage in the nineteenth century, or however old this paper was. The pattern was of thistles in shades of red.

A grand salon adjoined this room, with ten-foot ceilings embellished with floral molding and a large chandelier, which hung from a medallion in the center. The herringbone parquet floor was drenched in sunlight from tall windows on two sides of the room. More portraits of ancestors with eyes like Geoffrey's hung on walls papered in a more understated moss green wall covering with delicate gold pinstripes. The furnishings were delicate, too— eighteenth- and nineteenth-century parlor chairs and settees, and a large dining table. Obviously, this was the formal parlor.

You're missing this, Ma, I thought.

In fact, I'd been talking to her in my head since I walked through the door. Touring historic houses was a part of every vacation we ever took. Ma would lay her hand on a doorjamb of some Colonial home and say, "Think about it—George Washington may have touched this very spot!" We'd lay our own hands on the spot, wide-eyed. But those houses were museums with roped-off rooms; this was a living home where you could sit on the two-hundred-year-old furniture. Some part of my brain kept saying, *Look at this, Ma!* as if I didn't know how to experience this lovely old home without her.

I ran my hand over the smooth, cool mantel of the room's black marble fireplace, imagining the generations of hands that had done the same. How incredible to have grown up in a house like this. But then, my grandmother's house was old to us, too, nearly one hundred fifty years old, with fireplaces in every room—although they had been long sealed up. While the mantel in Geoffrey's house boasted a gold Empire-era clock, a white novelty cat terrine sat on Gramma's parlor fireplace. It had broken who knows when, and

Aunt Nicky had glued it with mucilage that turned black over the years, veining the cat's face and paws. Yet there it sat, just the same, year after year.

Across the room, an upright piano caught my eye. The finish on its elegant veneer had been worn away by age, or neglect, but the maker's name in gold lettering was still like new: C. MANGROT—PARIS. I played a chord on its ivory keys, but only a few notes sounded.

"It's very bad," Geoffrey said. "Very old."

A shame. There'd be no singalongs here. I wondered why they'd let it get so bad, something so beautiful.

The entire room was like this: in a state of decay. The wallpaper was stained from an old leak. The marble fireplace surround was cracking, as was the ceiling above. The floorboards were worn and spongy in places, the worst spots patched with duct tape.

There was something sad about it, but beautiful, too, more so for the fragility. Still elegant in spite of the wear, like an old woman in her favorite Chanel suit that had become tattered around the edges.

I told myself that if this were my house, I'd keep it just as it was, but Geoffrey's father had begun renovations to the room. Parts of the wallpaper had been ripped away, revealing even older wallpaper underneath. New windows had been installed, but the framing was still raw and unfinished.

Was it right or wrong to bust up something that had survived for so long? I couldn't bear to do it, but understood it needed doing. Things were crumbling, after all.

The cost and work to maintain a big, old chateau like this must be staggering. Would it be more curse than gift for Geoffrey to inherit this? Ma's childhood home had needed constant patching, too. Not all the renovations were in keeping with the period, though, for example, the faceless picture window Grandpa installed in the 1960s, replacing the eight-foot double-hung windows from 1840. But people from "the old country" have a different view of the past, a less precious view. When the past is all around you, it becomes more commonplace. There's nothing charming about a cracking mantel or a crumbling plaster ceiling when you're living with it. It's a safety hazard to be dealt with. You shake your fist at that old thing, want to rip it out. Maybe this is one of those examples of the past being more burden than treasure, but I still loved every crumbly bit of it.

"Come, Liza," Geoffrey said, "I want to show you where you stay."

As we climbed the stairs to the various levels of the house, Geoffrey pointed out the rooms. One, his father's art studio, a spacious atelier with a drafting desk under a skylight, where a still life of white peonies was just begun. And another room, up a short flight of stairs: "That's the dick."

Huh?

"I show you after lunch."

Okay. Whatever the dick was, I'd see it later.

The bedrooms were off a large, open landing where a skylight had recently been installed. My room was all in blue—blue wallpaper, blue ginger jar lamps, a blue Oriental rug, blue bedspread. The room was as large as the art studio, with an oversize window facing the garden.

"For you, Liza," Geoffrey said. "We call it the Blue Room."

Emotion gripped my throat. "You know blue is my favorite color, right?"

"I know!" Geoffrey said. "And your mother's, too."

Yes. Blue for Saint Mary. Always one room in blue.

We dropped my bag and then joined the family, who were gathered around the table in the garden, nibbling from small plates: olives, sausages, and goose liver wrapped in pastry, called *pâté en croute*. The others were filling their glasses from bottles set on a tray like a makeshift bar. There was rosé, sangria, Chablis, and, among these, an unmarked magnum of something they'd yet to open.

Geoffrey's mother motioned to a chair, saying the same words I'd heard all my life: "Sit! Eat! Drink!"

"Geoffrey, you don't sit," she said. "You help Mama." She beckoned him to follow her to the small house. They returned with more platters of food. The main course.

Plates were filled and passed off. Glasses were refilled. Hunks of bread were cut from a huge, crusty loaf. The conversation whipped around the table, everyone laughing and talking over one another. It was impossible to keep up with what they were saying, but it didn't matter. It was enough just to be in these beautiful surroundings, in jovial company. To be a part of their lives.

Geoffrey's father picked up the unmarked magnum that had been sitting unopened and offered me some of whatever was inside. Before I could say yes or no, a deep ruby liquid was filling my glass, a local vintage from a neighbor's *cave*.

"You have to see your face!" Geoffrey said, showing me the photo he'd just taken: me, looking up at that huge bottle with wide, shining eyes and a toothy grin across my face.

Just here a little over an hour, I was already happier than I'd been in seven weeks.

I announced that I would be staying another day.

"You want to see the dick?"

There was that word again. "The dick?"

"Yeah, you gotta see the dick. You want to see it?"

"Uh, sure, honey. Show me the dick." Knowing Geoffrey as I did, and his legendary "isms," I was pretty sure it wasn't what it sounded like.

Geoffrey, Christophe, and I climbed the stairs in the big house to the landing where he'd first shown me where the "dick" was. He opened the door and let me pass inside.

We were under the roof of the house, sunlight filtering in through the slats in the terra cotta roof tiles, the swirls of dust in the air illuminated like little galaxies. Old furniture, books, storage closets, and shelves filled the space, which looked like it spanned the entire length of the house.

"Attic," I said.

Geoffrey looked over at me. "What?"

"It's called an *attic*. Not a dick."

Geoffrey stared blankly. Christophe enlightened his husband, his body shaking with laughter as he shared the joke. For a guy who never spoke a word of English, I was starting to think Christophe understood more than he let on. Much more.

I was also pretty sure we'd be calling the attic the "dick" from now on, regardless.

The attic was filled, like all attics, with castoffs from prior generations, except here in France, in a three-hundred-year-old home, the castoffs were treasures, and not just for sentimental reasons. A nineteenth-century gold mantel mirror in pristine condition casually leaned against the wall. It would fetch several hundred euros easily at the Saint-Ouen antiques market. Tucked in a dark corner by the door: a nine-foot-tall walnut Louis XV wardrobe with beveled mirrored doors.

This was antique heaven, and they had it all tucked away in the dust and dark. Would it be rude to offer to buy that armoire, considering I'd arrived just a few hours ago?

Farther on, even more treasures were casually strewn about. A shaft of sunlight fell upon a pile of wooden chairs stripped of their cushions, legs in the air every which way—a heap of lovely, delicate bones. A few were nearly two hundred years old. The Ma in my head was bugging her eyes out at me. She and I had traversed acres of antique fairs, ogling priceless antiques like these, and here they had been just tossed aside.

My heart ached for these forgotten treasures. Such a waste. I wanted to gather all these things up, dust them off, and love them.

Did the family realize what they had up here? Or was it just so much old junk to a family with an institutional memory that spanned several generations?

There were some modern trinkets among the treasures, things from the early twentieth century: old vases, figurines, platters, clocks, and such. These were stored on shelves draped in plastic. Geoffrey's family seemed to care more for the objects of the recent past, items that triggered the most memories for them, than a whole room of history, much of which had probably been up here their entire lives, devoid of life.

I had a large storage unit in New Jersey filled with items like these, from Gramma's house, from Ma's. Bric-a-brac, mostly. None of it worth much, monetarily speaking, but that's not the point of saving a possession in an attic. It's there because you're not ready to part with it for whatever reason. The attic is a kind of purgatory for your past—still part of your story, hidden away but very much present. And in this attic in Burgundy, I could see the story of Geoffrey's family unfolding—by what they kept and how they kept it. Maybe that's why Geoffrey wanted me to see this. Being inside the attic was like being inside the owners' heads, their collective memory.

Was this why I felt so fragile when I saw all these neglected treasures, so like my own languishing in the storage facility I hadn't visited in a year? Why I wanted to rescue them? These chairs, these trinkets, these grand old armoires lived and breathed and spoke to me.

I've never been able to separate stuff from life.

A recurring nightmare plagues me: I'm on a train or a bus, and my stop is approaching. Suddenly I notice my personal belongings strewn about everywhere—in the aisle, on people's seats. Items of my favorite clothing, my makeup. Sometimes it's more precious things, such as an album of family photos or my favorite teacups from Gramma's house. I'm frantically gathering up everything and shoving it in my bag before my stop comes, but there's more and more.

"Stuff dreams," as I call them, usually happen when I'm anxious or stressed. I awake with my heart pounding. My stuff, unsafe in a strange place? Worst nightmare ever.

Gathering things close makes me feel safe. When I'm caring for old things I'm less fragile and helpless. Cherishing someone's cast-offs is about as useful as I can be.

Ma used to say when I was a kid that I loved my dolls more than I loved her, but of course, the dolls were easy to love; I could control them, how they treated me. But Ma was wrong about my loving them more than her. The dolls were just how I expressed my love. I became attached to things as a safe way of attaching to people.

My connection to the stuff of our family, and the nostalgia of the past, had been a way of dealing with the present. But maybe the reason I hadn't visited the storage unit in New Jersey, where all these treasures were stowed, was because a part of me was already moving on.

The village of Vézelay is on the top of a hill overlooking the valleys and towns in the area. It's a favorite tourist destination, as is its eleventh-century basilica. It was also just a thirty-minute walk from Geoffrey's town.

We set off from the house—Christophe, Geoffrey, his cousins, and I—and started our hike toward the hill town through Geoffrey's little village, a tight cluster of a hundred or so small stone homes, and other structures, all beautifully preserved. But all that preservation seemed to rob the town of a vital present. There was no real village life that I could see. The butcher, while he still lived in the town, according to Geoffrey, had closed up shop years before. And the grocery had never reopened after the owner died. The old building stood shuttered, same as the butcher shop, its hand-painted sign still visible on the side of the building, a reminder of a simpler time: C. GOURLET PRODUITS ALIMENTAIRES, TELEPHONE NO. 4.

Nowadays everyone preferred to drive to Avallon, to the Auchan, a French megastore like Walmart or Costco. The only commerce in town was a small *bar-tabac* with a couple of gas pumps outside. That was still pretty busy. A few of the patrons having a beer at one of the outside tables waved to Geoffrey as we walked by.

In the center of town was a large stone cross beside a tree in a grassy patch where the road forked. I asked what the cross was for—had someone died, or was it a war memorial? I'd seen another cross near Geoffrey's home that honored the fallen village sons of World War I.

Geoffrey shrugged. "There are a lot of crosses here."

As we continued up the road on our trek to Vézelay, I began to notice brass scallop shells embedded every few yards or so. They were all very highly polished, as if someone walked along buffing them weekly. "Pretty. What are these for?"

Geoffrey pointed to the street sign: CHEMIN DE SAINT-JACQUES. "It's why there are a lot of crosses. Saint Jacques de Compostelle."

I was walking the Saint James Trail.

Being raised Catholic, I'd known about this, but had never seen it. The trail goes all over Europe. Catholic pilgrims have followed it for centuries, walking on foot or sometimes on their knees, like Saint James. Geoffrey's town is part of the route, and Vézelay, according to Geoffrey, is where it starts in France.

Of all the towns in France, I was in one of the most important spiritual sites for Catholics, a place of salvation—my mother still pulling the strings up there, perhaps, guiding me on my spiritual journey.

The trail was uphill all the way, under the relentless afternoon sun, but our surroundings provided the consolation prize. Blackberries and wildflowers lined the road, farmland spread out on either side, dotted by cows and sheep munching contentedly on lush grasses. At every fork, a cross sprouted up, stones and shells laid at its base, offerings from religious pilgrims.

"They call this road le Chemin des Américains," Geoffrey said.

It wasn't the real name but what the villagers had called it ever since American troops used it to drive out the Nazis seventy years before. "The American Way."

A route of salvation in a place of salvation. This American had her very own road for her very own pilgrimage. I'd started out bravely the day I decided to leave my job, but I'd faltered along the way, been tested. Lost faith. Here in Burgundy I was being given signs, glimpses of the familiar, reminders of family, which fortified me as I pushed onward. Under the sun in this spiritual place, on a road of liberation named for my countrymen, I knew everything that had happened to me had been meant to be. Even the difficult times. Especially those.

Geoffrey took us off the main path, to his favorite childhood shortcut, straight up the hill along rocky trails through the woods. In the heat. This pilgrim would really have to suffer before she got to heaven, stopping twice to catch her breath. Several weeks of sitting and writing, eating cheese and bread, had taken their toll.

The reward awaited us at the top of the hill: limitless views in all directions. We rested on a stone bench, looking out over Geoffrey's village, the farms and vineyards in the valley, squares of different textures and shades of green taking our breath away even as we were trying to catch it. From this vantage point, I could trace the road we'd just traveled back toward the house. I liked seeing how far I'd come.

The Basilica of Saint Mary Magdalene was perched at the highest point of the hill, surrounded by imposing stone fortifications protecting it from intruders. Inside the wall, though, the medieval village was full of warmth and life, with inviting cobblestone streets lined with cheerful shops and town houses—doors and shutters painted in pastel blues, pinks, and greens. Though filled with tourists, it didn't feel touristy; it hadn't surrendered itself to the trappings of the trade, naïvely retaining its simple village ways, real and humble, as if surprised tourists found it interesting at all.

Maybe the humility was born of its spiritual roots, and the religious pilgrims who came here less to buy trinkets than to find meaning in the simple surroundings.

We explored the hilly, narrow streets, ate ice cream, sipped drinks at a café overlooking the valley—simple pleasures in a simple place.

I wanted to see the basilica and light a candle for Ma. I'd lit candles for her in a lot of churches during these weeks in France. Funny how even though I was no longer a practicing Catholic, I still sought solace in churches when I felt vulnerable and alone. I even prayed at the most desperate times, sobbed in pews all over Paris. Maybe I just wanted to feel a connection to Ma when I needed her most.

The Romanesque façade of the basilica was austere and foreboding, like the fortifications around the town. And like the fortifications, the façade hid a joyful interior: a bright, white space with a lofty vaulted ceiling, the apse the brightest point, with rays of light shining on the altar from windows high above. You'd never know how many wars, invasions, revolts, and fires it had gone through. The violence had only purged it, made it purer, more beautiful.

Like the town itself, there was no flash—no gilt statues, no polished marble or frescoes of angels. No show of opulence at all. A simple wooden bench stood in for the altar, a crisp linen cloth laid across.

There was nothing here to distract you from your spiritual quest.

Geoffrey led me to the center of the nave, to a few stairs that descended under the floor, where the crypt was. He pointed to a reliquary: "Saint Marie-Magdalene."

Now I knew why Vézelay was the starting point of the Saint James Trail in France. Even a nonpracticing Catholic was obliged to be awestruck. *Oh, Ma!* As saints go, Mary Magdalene was my personal patron because, unlike what they taught us in Sunday school, I knew she was really an important and powerful woman. And the man who stowed her relics for safekeeping during the French Revolution had nearly the same name as my father: Joseph-Philippe d'Anselmo. Here I was in her last resting place, completely by chance.

Oh, who was I kidding? *Message received, Ma.*

Before we left, I lit a candle for my mother, but for the first time in weeks, it wasn't because I felt vulnerable. I did it to celebrate this day.

I woke up to "Happy Birthday" being sung in French coming from somewhere downstairs.

Was I the last to rise? I threw myself together and followed the smell of coffee and toast to the kitchen. Everyone, minus Geoffrey's parents, was sitting at the table having breakfast.

"Hey!" Geoffrey greeted me, cup in one hand, toasted baguette in the other. "Sit. I get you breakfast."

The birthday boy, Christophe, was still sleepy-eyed, having just woken up, like me. I wished him a *Bon anniversaire* with cheek kisses. He gave me a sleepy *merci*.

They were toasting bread in an antique toaster that had a central heating coil and wire doors on either side that flipped out, designed for a baguette sliced lengthwise. Other than the coffee maker, it was the only cooking device left in the kitchen. The old wood-burning cast-iron stove had been pulled out, along with everything else from the former kitchen, except for the sink—an old porcelain basin fed by a spigot in the wall attached to exposed copper pipes. The white-and-blue tile backsplash from the nineteenth century also remained, as did the original blue walls. It was a strong blue, particular in hue, with the smallest hint of green, or maybe it was gray. As unique as this blue was, it was wholly familiar to me.

My mother called it "Williamsburg Blue," and painted our own kitchen this color in the 1980s, so named for Colonial Williamsburg, in Virginia, one of her favorite places. Ma loved all things Colonial America; I grew up surrounded by the décor and colors of that era.

Everywhere I turned in Geoffrey's family home I kept seeing something familiar, something that evoked a memory from the homes of my past, especially my grandmother's—from the color of the stain on the paneling to the way the old light switches were jerry-rigged. Even the smell was familiar, something soft and powdery like sachets and old wood. I never thought I'd smell that scent again. I walked around the house inhaling deep and long, holding it in, letting it refresh my memory.

We finished our breakfast and cleaned up the kitchen, everyone going his or her separate way. The cousins went for a hike; Geoffrey was going to bake Christophe's birthday cake with his mother. Christophe, a nurse with a grueling schedule, was happy to do nothing on his birthday.

It was just about filling the lull between breakfast and lunch, anyway.

Since the day I'd arrived in Burgundy, eating had been the main activity, everything focusing around lunch and dinner—and in between, we'd talk about what we were going to eat at the next meal. There was no grabbing a sandwich for lunch. We sat at the table in the garden for two hours. Dinners, which we had in the big house, were three hours or more—course after course, bottle after bottle. We didn't leave the table until it was time for bed.

Being in Burgundy, where life was slower and simpler, French food culture really came to life. Breakfast was bread and coffee. Anything more would spoil your lunch, which started around twelve thirty with the *apéro*, the point of which was to whet your appetite. The main component of this was the cocktail, often sweet, such as kir, which is white wine and crème de cassis, though, at this house, sangria was popular for summer.

You couldn't have a cocktail without something to nibble on, or it wouldn't be a proper *apéro*. Savory crackers or olives were common, but canapés were also served. Geoffrey's mother also made *gougères*, a traditional cheesy puff pastry from the Burgundy region.

The *apéro* is never, *ever* passed over. Even Parisians, with their busy lives, gather in the cafés after work for a drink and a snack before dinner. Now it made sense to me.

The main course followed, and the wine. In this case, we drank Burgundy, what else? Mâconnais, Chablis, Côte de Beaune—often from small, local vineyards.

There was no such thing as a light, summery main course here at the house. We had casseroles and roasts. Geoffrey's mother was a wonderful cook, like my mother, planning and cooking meal upon meal with ease. An endless stream of platters came out to the table, yet I swore I barely saw her in the kitchen.

You had to learn to pace yourself, because after the main course came the cheese. And with the cheese, more wine. Like the *apéro*, we never missed a cheese course. I counted seven types: goat, cow, runny, firm, bleu. We didn't polish them off in one sitting; we'd just have a sample of each; then the cheese platter would make another appearance at the next meal, replenished with whatever was finished in the last round.

Bread was served throughout. The huge, crusty loaf I'd first seen when I arrived never seemed to diminish. Like the cheese plate, it just kept showing up at every meal, Geoffrey's father cutting off chunks as needed—a miracle of the loaves right here in Burgundy. Maybe this was why people made pilgrimages here.

If you were full at this point, too bad—*tant pis*—because after the cheese came dessert. And after that, the coffee and liqueurs. One, an eau-de-vie called Mirabelle, was made from plums of the same name. In this case, *home*made. It packed a hell of a punch.

And this was just lunch.

We repeated this ritual for dinner, starting with the *apéro*, in the garden at around six o'clock. The main event was a candlelit affair in the grand salon, the dim light obscuring the decay, restoring the old *grande dame* to her elegant former self.

French food culture wasn't exactly foreign to me. I grew up with a similar relationship to food, sitting around tables for hours, too. At Christmas, we sat down at two o'clock in the afternoon and would not get up again until two o'clock in the morning.

Sitting in the garden at Christophe's birthday lunch, around a picnic table almost identical to Ma's, with its familiar plastic tablecloth, I could have been at my mother's annual Memorial Day party. Even the Pyrex baking dish with roasted chicken thighs was the same. All Christophe's cake needed was little American flag toothpicks stuck in it.

I realized how much I'd missed this.

My mother had held us all together. She'd gather us at her house, family, longtime friends, and in doing so, would keep me connected to a larger community. When she died, that connection was broken. I hadn't noticed this until now, because my life had become so inwardly focused. I'd wanted to be on my own, have only myself to worry about. But now it dawned on me that I didn't want that anymore. Life was hard enough, and much harder when you tried to go it alone. Why had I felt that I had to for so long?

Family, friends, and food—the French trinity. Wasn't this what mattered most?

La cave—pronounced "kahv"—is the right of every Frenchman, particularly if you live in wine country. Often subterranean, like a cellar, but not always, it is characterized by vaulted stone ceilings, barrels of wine, and in the best ones, a long table for drinking with friends.

Geoffrey's father took pride in showing me his *cave*. He used it to store his bottles of wine, and had set it up like a social club, with lounge chairs and party lights.

"Before you leave Burgundy, Liza, you will have to drink wine in a *cave*," he said.

I was on board with that plan, 100 percent. There is an episode of Anthony Bourdain's *No Reservations* that was shot in Burgundy, in which Bourdain drinks wine in a *cave* and sings French drinking songs. I envied the life that man had.

My opportunity to do like Bourdain came from a neighbor, a retired cop named Patrick, who invited us for *apéro* in his *cave*, where he made his own wine for personal consumption.

The family lived just up the road, a few minutes' walk, in a town house. We'd walked past the house many times, but we'd been deceived by its size. Once inside the gate, we entered a complex of buildings similar to Geoffrey's parents' property. The *cave* wasn't underground, so it was dry inside, probably ideal for making wine. A small window facing the street allowed slivers of sunlight to seep in, aided by a fluorescent light hanging from the arched ceiling.

Two large barrels lay on their sides along one wall, heavy with fermenting grape. Beside them, two small barrels created the perfect little family. Several bottle trees occupied the opposite wall—wire stands where empty wine bottles were hung upside down, waiting to be filled. The light filtered through the glass bottles, blue and green, creating Pop Art floor lamps for our wine den.

Patrick, a bear of a man with piercing blue eyes, syphoned wine from one of the larger barrels into a glass. The wine they were making right now was white.

"You want to try?" He held the glass out to me. It wasn't quite ready yet, he said, but worth a try.

"Sure!" I took it eagerly.

"Liza is great," Geoffrey said, "because she always says yes."

I do? Since when?

I held the glass up to the light. Buttery yellow, but a bit cloudy. Hmm . . . silt? Sediment? Eh, whatever. I took a sip. Everyone waited for my reaction. I expected the taste to be cloying, like the homemade wine Italian grandfathers make, but it was crisp and light, if a bit one-note. Patrick was right, not ready but totally drinkable. "Pas mal," I said. Not bad.

Everyone cheered, and passed their empty glasses to Patrick to be filled. We stood around among the barrels drinking wine. In a cave.

I wanted to shout, "I'm freaking Anthony Bourdain!" Except no one there would have understood, so I just screamed in my head as I sipped my wine while looking around at everyone sipping theirs. A year ago I was wishing I could do something like this. Had I gotten here by saying yes all the time? Did I really say it more than I knew?

"Hey, what's that drinking song?" I asked. "Where you sing, 'Et glou, et glou, et glou,' and touch the glass to your nose, or something?" I acted it out.

The others broke into the song instantly, glasses aloft, and then touched them to their foreheads, noses, chins—their bellowing voices filling the cave.

Bourdain had nothing on me right now.

Geoffrey took a photo of my face—and there was that same expression of delight.

"Do you know 'rata'?" Patrick asked me. He pointed to the smaller barrels. One was labeled RATA 13, I assumed for the vintage.

"No, what is it?"

"Oh, you have to try!" Geoffrey's mother said. "Ratafia. It's good!"

Patrick took my wineglass, dumped out what was left, and refilled it with ratafia. It was a little deeper in color than the wine. He said this batch was made with something called "coing."

As soon as he said that word, everyone wanted a taste.

"Coing, c'est quoi?" I asked. What was this stuff?

Patrick opened a large plastic bin and pointed inside.

A dark, lumpy, gelatinous substance gave off an acrid, pungent odor I'd become all too familiar with lately.

Others peeked and took a whiff, too. They were as sorry as I. This made something that tasted good?

I sniffed at the liquid in my glass. None of the must, just a hint of fruit. I took a sip. Strong, crisp, smooth, and dry. "It's quince! Delicious."

"You see?" Geoffrey's mother said.

Patrick's smile spread. "Like it?" He took a bottle from a shelf— dark green and covered in dust, the cork sealed by hand with a drop of red wax. "For you."

He gave me a nod, winked one of his blue eyes. Grabbing a few more bottles from the shelf, he motioned for us to move the party outside.

Patrick's wife had set up the *apéro* in the garden. A few other neighbors had showed up and were sitting around in folding chairs, chatting. Patrick filled all our glasses with rata.

A huge spread of appetizers had been laid out. One plate contained long, thin shavings of a cured meat. They were putting it on bread with butter. Patrick offered it to me.

The impish delight in the eyes of those around me was mixed with a dash of *Let's see what the little American is made of*. I took a bite, and received nods of approval all around.

"What is it?" I asked.

"Wild boar!" Geoffrey laughed. "Liza has a man inside," he said in French. "She is so brave. She'll try anything."

My Paris friends thought of me as bold. It made sense. Paris drew it out of me. But it didn't take a huge amount of courage to try cured boar. A stronger, more concentrated flavor than the domestic variety, but not as gamey as I'd have thought. "Mais, c'est vachement bon."

Vache means "cow," so *vachement* literally means "cowly," but it's used as a superlative. Basically I'd said, "It's oh-my-God-like-super-totally good," which made Geoffrey and Christophe burst out laughing.

"Ah, but you're so Frenchy, my Liza!" Geoffrey said. "Your

French is perfect now!" But when he repeated what I'd said to the group, he added a *putain*, as in "Putain, c'est vachement bon."

"Hey, I never said, 'putain'!" I protested, laughing. "I would never say 'putain' in front of your parents."

"But you can!" Geoffrey's mother said. She made me another wild boar and butter sandwich.

I guess I was family now.

By the time the sun had set, several other neighbors had stopped by, swelling our party to about a dozen. We polished off four bottles of ratafia.

"We do this every day," Geoffrey's mother told me. "At a different house each night." They took turns in the village, hosting *apéro*. Every day. What a life.

"I'm going to stay another day," I said.

On the morning of my last day in Burgundy, I dreamed about my old job. In the dream, I was back in the office, where I was supposed to be working on a freelance project, but nobody would talk to me; they bustled about with barely a notice of my existence. The freelance offer had dried up, and when I protested to my old boss and friend, she just shrugged and smiled. "I know, but there's nothing we can do," she said. "It's just the way it is." They'd promised me freelance work; I'd counted on it to keep myself afloat. My safety net was gone. *Well, that's it*, I told myself in the dream, *you're really going to have to make a go of your new life. Because this one is done.*

I awoke wistful but resolute.

Geoffrey and I took a long walk under the early morning sun through the village and the countryside. I took photographs, snatches of memory of this intoxicating place: morning glory vines clinging to a stone wall, a weathered blue door, a cork left on a window sill, one of the brass scallop shells embedded in the road.

The mist still hung on the horizon, turning the landscape and the basilica on the hill in Vézelay into cutouts in a diorama, the distance defined by flat shades of green, bright to pale.

We walked along a dirt road through fields and farmland, beside a river called La Cure, and again I was struck by how familiar it felt, how much like the roads I'd hiked as a kid in our rural town. Everything here triggered memories of home, mostly of what I'd lost—but instead of bringing pain, it healed me.

I'd ended up staying two extra days in this place of cure, soaking up the simple pleasures of life. Burgundy had lifted me up and brought me back to earth at the same time. Back to myself—making me stronger, and teaching me what mattered most. I had been a pilgrim, traveling far for salvation and meaning, and I'd found it in a place that felt like home.

During the last three years I'd been filling the hole my mother's death left in my world, finding my own purpose, and I'd done a good job growing my new life. But there was one thing that hadn't grown in, a hole my days in Burgundy filled temporarily: a life where family was at the center.

Burgundy made me realize that for all my ambitions of a bigger life, a new career, travel, nothing made me happier or more at peace than just being with the people I loved, sharing the simple pleasures. If I could create my life around that, even if I never achieved the big successes, I'd probably die happy.

I had been running away or toward something else besides my pain, but now I wanted to come home to a life surrounded by friends and family, as Ma had done. To be attached, to belong, and to celebrate my life with those I loved.

PART 5

Sharing My Paris Life

· Seventeen ·

Celebrating My Life in Paris

Paris had been my sanctuary from the world in many ways, and I kept it separate from my New York life. Like my bedroom as a kid, it was the one place where I felt free to create the life I wanted for myself. I had needed that buffer from those who knew me too well, who could name my flaws, because I'd convinced myself my family's presence in Paris might have squashed my delicate dream—the familiar criticisms mirroring my own fears and limitations, like a big alarm clock waking me up. *Who do you think you are?*

But my Paris life wouldn't be truly happy, or complete, if I didn't bring my whole world together in it—Paris *and* New York. Only then would Paris really be home to me.

It was October, and I'd arrived a few days ahead of my family to get everything ready for their arrival. October is a wonderful month in Paris. The weather is still fine, and you can find a street flea market or autumn festival almost every weekend. It's the perfect time to plan a week of events for a birthday celebration, and definitely better than December, when my real birthday is.

There was a reason October had been my first choice. The day that kicked off the party week was Ma's birthday.

The invitees: my sister, Maria; my childhood friend Steven, and his wife, Virginia; my dear New York friend Matthew with his boy-friend, Frank. My family.

Steven's family and mine had celebrated every major holiday and life event together since he and I were young. With our own relatives far away in Buffalo, we adopted our neighbors. Christmas, Easter, birthdays, Mother's Day, Memorial Day, Fourth of July—we were never four; we were a family of eight. Steven spent more time in my house than in his own, as did his sister. We four were like siblings, as close as the real thing. Spouses increased our number.

Steven's daughters call my sister and me Aunt Maria and Aunt Lisa. He and my mother had been as close as mother and son, and he missed her as deeply as Maria and I did. He'd often text us pictures of one of her recipes he'd made for dinner, nostalgic for her cooking.

Both he and Virginia had dreamed of my mother a few months before the Paris trip. In their dreams, Ma was with us in my apartment. In Virginia's dream, it was Ma who greeted them at the door when they arrived, scolding, "What took you so long?"

Steven and Virginia were arriving from New Jersey around the same time as my sister, who was flying in from Miami. I'd sent a car for them, prepared lunch. Then I waited impatiently, nervously.

My two worlds were about to collide: familiar New York meeting exotic Paris; my history smack in the middle of my future. Would it be weird? Would it bring my old baggage into my new home?

The instant I heard Steven's voice over the intercom any fears I had evaporated. Seconds later, my family was at the door of my Paris life.

"What took you so long?" I said, channeling Ma.

They burst into the apartment, my sister carrying a huge bouquet she'd bought on the way from the hotel, which was just up the street. They were all talking at once—about the ride over in the taxi, how nice the hotel was, how beautiful the flowers in the shop were. They gushed over my petite home, took pictures of every facet as if it were a tourist attraction. I just stood there, smiling. This wasn't weird at all. This was wonderful.

Sharing the joy of my Paris life was already having a halo effect on my family. Steven was transformed instantly; I could see the stress and fatigue melting from his face. His energy bloomed. Virginia, too, was more gregarious than usual. My sister seemed right at home, totally at peace. She had brought some homemade treats to share with us, her way of blessing the house just as Ma might have done. Everything seemed right, as though it had always been this way. What had I been so afraid of?

All my life I'd been protecting myself from the effects of others. Whether it was my bedroom door or a too-busy schedule, I always put something between myself and those close to me. I'd even joked that the quality of my relationship with my sister was in direct proportion to the number of miles between us. That seemed unthinkable now. But how much of that was self-protection and how much was insecurity—being afraid to reveal something flawed about myself if I got too close?

What about my effect on other people? I was being stingy with myself, and missing out on a chance to have an impact, significance. My Paris life was making others happy, those closest to me. Could it heal them, too? They'd also lost Ma; her death hadn't happened to me alone. I'd been focused on myself and my own pain, but what about theirs?

After lunch we stayed in my neighborhood for "Lisa's Paris Life Tour," as Steven called it. I showed them the banal details of my daily routine—*Here's my market. Here's where I go for happy hour. This is where that hot wine guy works.* Things I took for granted made them goggle-eyed: the pharmacies, the Métro stations, the flower shops. Maria loved how my quartier felt, "local and homey, like your neighborhood in New York." Again, they snapped photos of everything. I imagined their friends looking at these images later, wondering why a Franprix supermarket was so riveting.

Being able to show them the life I'd built, having them bear witness, made it more real. Watching them discover my district reminded me that what I had accomplished *was* something exciting. With everything that had happened in recent months, the leak in my apartment that *still* leaked, I'd forgotten the thrill of my life here. With each piece of my life I shared with my family, the more euphoric I became.

What if Ma could have come back for this one day with all of us—walk around with us, share in my Paris life? What would this day have been like? What would *her* validation have felt like, the one person I'd always needed it from most?

Did I still need it?

When Ma was in the oncology ward and I was talking about the trip to Paris we would take together that coming April, she nodded along, even telling her visiting friends about it. When she was better, she had said, we'd go. But I wonder if she just agreed to it for me, if she knew she was dying and that I was the one who really needed the LFT—the "Look Forward To." Did she know her daughter was drowning at the thought of losing her, and was she just throwing me a lifeline?

I had gone so far as to book a flight for us, and reserve a room at my favorite hotel. Finally, Ma would see my Paris with me.

She would die only three weeks later. I used those airline tickets for my sister and me, so we could spend that first Christmas without Ma in Paris.

Now, having the four of us together, Maria, Steven, Virginia, and me, would be as close to having Ma with us in Paris as we could get. But we felt her presence among us—her "kids," as she called us all, as if she had four children, not just two.

We celebrated Ma's birthday in a small bistro on rue Alexandre-Dumas. We were alone in the restaurant for a long time, as if we were meant to have a private moment to reflect. We toasted Ma, the clinking of our champagne glasses like the sealing of a pact: we would always be together.

Things didn't stay rosy forever.

Virginia wanted to visit Saint-Pierre de Montmartre, so she and I set out early together. It was a gorgeous morning, the start of what was forecast to be another warm, sunny day.

The plan: to have lunch at one of my old haunts in the 18th arrondissement, away from the touristy Butte Montmartre, on rue Caulaincourt. Maria was sleeping in at the hotel; Steven would pick her up after a private cooking lesson and join us there. Matthew and Frank, who'd arrived a few days after the others, wanted to walk from their rental apartment in the Marais. I warned them that it was an uphill hike, but they said they didn't mind.

Everyone had confirmed before they went off on their separate ways, but when I texted Matthew to see where he was, and to give him the address of the restaurant, he didn't like my lunch arrangements. They were already on the top of Montmartre and had been touring around. They were hot and hungry. Could we change the plan?

Change the plan?

A muscle in my back tightened. I'd spent weeks planning the trip, organizing the activities for each day, and I was beginning to feel the pressure. When Matthew and Frank were added to the group, it had required a lot of energy to get everyone together, to manage all the personalities, find things everyone liked. Since it was my town, I felt responsible for keeping everyone happy, and making sure they were taken care of. Nobody asked for that; it was just something I needed to do.

And I needed everyone to cooperate. Okay, people?

Virginia and I caught up with Matthew and Frank at the top of the hill in Montmartre. We managed to find a terrace table at a family-owned café just down the hill from the Basilica of Sacré-Coeur—a cute place, but, unlike the café I'd originally chosen, this was buried deep in the middle of the winding, hilly web of streets that is Montmartre. I poke-poke-poked at the map program on my phone, looking for the best way to direct Steven and Maria, who were already on the Métro headed to another station farther away.

"They're grown-ups," Matthew said. "They'll find us. Relax."

Oh, yeah, sure. He'd screwed it all up, but I was the problem? "They don't have data on their phones here, Matthew. Meaning no map programs." *Poke-poke-poke.* "It's not as easy as you think."

How would I get Maria safely to me? Maybe I should have stuck to my guns and made Matthew and Frank come to us at the other café. At least they would have been walking downhill. Steven and Maria would be climbing steep lanes all the way. Maria was going to be furious with me for making her tramp all over the place. This was a nightmare!

I was the girl with the broom again, furiously sweeping, keeping things tidy and orderly. I could feel it coming on slowly after a few days: the spinning. Whenever Maria complained about something, however personal it was, I felt the need to fix it. Each time Matthew second-guessed a plan, it sent me scrambling to keep things on track. They were all just being themselves; this was nothing new. It was the usual family dynamics.

Chaos, in Paris.

This was my city, my world, created my way. Now I'd let these people in it, with their agendas and needs, and they were making me nuts.

Or was that me making myself nuts?

You can always count on family to take you right back to childhood, just when you think you've worked through all your issues. Buttons were being pushed all over the place, and once again, there I was trying to control the family dynamics impacting me by controlling everyone and everything.

Matthew was right about everyone being grown-ups. They were going to be however they were going to be. I needed to let go and let them be themselves—complain if they wanted; go off on their own if they wanted. Why did I feel I had to be the mama bear? Did I think their happiness was my responsibility?

Whoa—I did think that.

Part of my mind was still fixated on my mother looking at herself in the mirror and hating her reflection. And that part had been controlling me all my life—until now.

It wasn't my fault Ma had been unhappy. It wasn't my fault when she threw a tantrum and created chaos in my world. But eight-year-old Lisa truly believed if things fell apart at home, she had failed.

I had been the parent to Ma's wounded child—assuaging, soothing, taking responsibility for her. I put that weight on my shoulders as a child and then carried it with me all these years.

I was exhausted.

With one shrug, I dumped that weight from my shoulders and freed myself. Enough.

I was among people I loved—it's what I wanted, wasn't it?—each with his or her own personality and, yes, they'd tweak a nerve now and again, but their issues were theirs. It wasn't personal to me; it didn't need to affect me. There was no need to run around pleasing everyone, managing their moods, moderating every potential conflict. Not my job.

I was not the one holding it all together, and if I stopped spinning, the world would not come to an end. Control didn't make me important, or needed, or worthy. That I breathed made me worthy. So I just sat in that café, let go, and breathed.

My sister and Steven found us at the restaurant with little problem. Maria arrived chattering about how cute everything was, how much she liked the pretty cobbled lanes. We ended up having a wonderful lunch on the hill, maybe even nicer than the one we might have had at my original choice. We were all content, fed, and pleasantly buzzed on good French wine. That was the goal, anyway. I forgave Matthew for throwing a monkey wrench into my plans; I was actually grateful for it. My plans had needed shaking up, and so had I.

That night, we gathered together in my apartment for a light supper, and I uncorked the bottle of ratafia Patrick had given me in Burgundy six weeks before.

I took a photo of everyone sitting together in the living room—a photo I'd taken many times before of my Paris friends. It was identical in every way, except the faces were of those I'd known three times longer, who knew me three times better.

Having my family in Paris was the opposite of what I'd feared: their presence made my life here more real. Keeping Paris in its own compartment had prevented me from fully embracing it. Paris wasn't just part of my life, even though I spent part of my time here; it had become the center of my universe, my identity. Sharing Paris with others was the same as sharing myself.

I'm in our childhood home again. I know this dream. Our things are still inside, but we don't own it anymore. I panic and try to quickly pack up our precious belongings. Not again. Why do I have to keep packing up this stuff over and over? They're coming, the new owners. They're coming, and we shouldn't be here; we're trespassing. Why are we still here?

I'd been having this dream since we sold the house; I was having it again here in Paris while my family was visiting. I knew it was a dream while I was having it, but I couldn't get out of it. This was the most agonizing of all my "Stuff Dreams," and it wouldn't go away.

But this time the dream was different. I'm in the house with Steven and Virginia. Maria is in her room with the door closed. Virginia's family is here to help us empty the house, but they're giving away things I don't want given away. I become hysterical, ranting and crying. Then it hits me: something is wrong.

"We've already done this," I tell Steven. A calm falls over me. "I'll show you." I concentrate hard and wave my hand. The room we're in, the living room, is suddenly empty of all its contents.

"And we renovated." I wave my hand again. "This is what it looks like." The room is transformed: walls painted in a warm beige with the crown molding we added, floor polished bright. I go around, from room to room, and do the same, taking Steven and Virginia with me.

"Don't tell Maria," I say. "I'll do her room last. I don't want to upset her."

I break the news to Maria, and we walk through the house, now empty and renovated. I remind my sister that the pain is behind us. Together we transform the last room, hers. It empties, becomes freshly painted.

"This is how the house is now," I say. "It's done. It's all done."

The new owners come into the house, and it transforms again: their furniture and trinkets appear. They've even added an addition off the dining room.

They give us a tour, proud and happy of their new home. The house looks nothing like ours anymore, but it's lovely, and I tell them so. "Enjoy this house," I say, totally at peace and filled with joy. "It's yours now."

The sommelier popped the champagne cork and filled our glasses. The chef, a friend of mine, mouthed "Happy birthday" from his open galley kitchen facing the high-top table where I sat surrounded by my family and closest friends.

Family, friends, and food—and Paris.

This was a gift I gave myself, to gather together everyone I loved in the city I loved, bringing everything full circle. We ate seven courses, polished off six bottles of wine, stayed long after closing, dancing with the staff of the restaurant. Everyone talked about how special this was, how they'd never forget this amazing night. And that was my gift to them.

After Ma died, I ran away to Paris, away from anything that reminded me how miserable I was, how lost I felt. And Paris gave me what I needed then, taught me to hope and dared me to go farther than I thought I could go, to live bigger than I'd ever lived. Paris had healed me, not by making me stronger—I realized I was strong at the start—but by breaking me down and teaching me to be vulnerable and open.

All my life I'd been keeping myself stowed away, afraid to put myself out there, to connect with the world in a bigger way. It wasn't just about protecting myself from others; I was also protecting others from me—the real me. I was afraid that if they really knew me, if they saw my worthless reflection in the mirror, they'd realize I was a fraud and kick me out of their paradise.

But standing in front of that mirror now, nearly three years after Ma died, I saw reflected back someone who *had* put herself out there—bought an apartment in Paris; left a safe, cushy job for an uncharted future. I was miles from where I was then, and it happened with a first step, a single thought: *I deserve to be happy.*

"Happy birthday, Lee," my sister said, hugging me and planting a huge red lipstick kiss on my cheek. "I'm so proud of you."

"For what?"

"For this. For Paris. Ma would have been proud, too."

Ma. Even in the face of her own sense of worthlessness, she had inspired me. Through her dreams, she showed me there was more to life, and taught me to seek the highest—even if she couldn't show me how to reach for it. That was for me to discover. And I did it in Paris.

French Consulate, Upper East Side, New York City

The snow on East Seventy-fourth Street was still fluffy and pristine, what you'd expect from the swanky Upper East Side. It hung on the trees and windowsills, crunched under my boots. A few flakes floated down from low, gray clouds.

The security guard at the door of the converted brownstone asked for my ID, searched my bag, and told me to pass through the metal detector. "That's where you go." He pointed to a long line that snaked up the stairs to the second level.

Inching my way along, step by step up the stairs, I finally reached the head of the line. "Next person!" a woman behind a bulletproof window called out in a thick French accent.

I stepped up to the window, handed her my receipt of payment, proof I'd been through the grueling interview process. She disappeared for a minute and returned with my passport, which they'd held hostage for two weeks.

"Check zuh spelling of your name, please."

I opened the passport to the page she'd marked. "It's correct."

"Bon. Merci. We welcome you in France, madame."

Back out in the snowy street, I opened my passport to look at it again. After three months of paperwork, of getting recommendation letters and FBI documents, of building my professional dossier, the result was finally in my hands. I ran my finger over the engraved letters: *V-I-S-A*.

My long-term-stay visa for France had been granted.

From here, who knew? There would be no plans or safety nets, and no guarantees—nothing to limit my thinking or contain who I would become.

The story would write itself starting now.

Acknowledgments

I have a friend who likes to play a game of career provenance with me, tracing the person who'd hired us at our current position all the way back to the first person who had (unwittingly) set everything in motion. As we'd identify each person involved, and how they were connected to the person who came before, a chain of gratitude was created.

My memoir has a gratitude provenance like this, with many having a hand in its coming about. Starting with the present and my editor, Kat Brzozowski.

Kat is a true writer's editor, that is to say the kind of editor from out of the 1950s who plucks a writer from obscurity and works with her to bring her manuscript to fruition. That kind of editor is rare today, and I'm acutely aware of how lucky I am. She took a huge chance on me, and I'm thankful for that—and for her—every day.

With Kat's fierce intelligence and her ability to distill the story down to its most potent elements, she guided me through what felt like an impossible task: writing a memoir about something while it was still fresh and raw. I wasn't sure I had anything to say, but Kat saw it differently, encouraging me and drawing out (or should I say dragging?) the deeper story from me. She was better than a psychologist at making me examine my past in a brutally honest way. I often broke down sobbing as I typed—cursing Kat for making me go there. But damn, if she wasn't right. It was worth every tear.

This book is the fruit of our labor, born of a true partnership, with Kat investing huge amounts of time and energy into the book and its author. I owe her everything.

But Kat may never have found me if not for an article written by Tim Murphy for *New York*, part of a thirty-day blog on Paris. Tim interviewed me about my life between New York and Paris, and included a link to my blog, *My (Part-Time) Paris Life*. I received more than six thousand hits on my blog the day the article was released and told Tim I owed him a drink. The next day he forwarded me an email from Kat. Now I owe him a whole lot more.

How did I meet Tim? Through the next person on my gratitude chain: Lapo Belmestieri, who recommended me for the article. Lapo appears in this memoir and is someone who continually nudges—and sometimes shoves—me outside my comfort zone. It was Lapo who said the magic words that encouraged me to take the leap of faith and change my life. That pivotal moment appears in these pages.

But I wouldn't know Lapo if not for Matthew Waldman, also in this book. For more than twenty years, Matthew has been my New York brother, and I rely on his candor, wit, and wisdom—possibly too much. He is always there to celebrate my every success—like this book, for which he even sketched cover ideas. In one, I'm riding the Eiffel Tower like a pony while wearing a cowboy hat. He was really keen on that one, but as you can see, it didn't make the cut. So for my friend, I've written that idea here, as a way of saying "thank you."

As it turns out, Matthew and I were brought together by the same woman who taught me to play this game of provenance. Her name is Lucy Sisman, and she was one of my first bosses when I was still a young designer. With Lucy, I worked on the launch of

Allure magazine, and that led to every other job I've ever had, including the one I write about in this book. Lucy raised the bar of excellence for me and taught me that there is nothing that cannot be done. This has defined me for the last twenty-five years.

I met Lucy through a creative director for whom I was freelancing, who was married to the director of another magazine where I had worked the year before. And I got *that* job thanks to a fellow student at Parsons School of Design. But I would not have gone to Parsons if not for the insistence of one person: my mother.

So the provenance of this memoir traces back to the woman who features so prominently in its pages. Without realizing it, my mother set about the chain of events that would ultimately lead to her daughter's first published book.

Thank you, Ma. Wherever you are.

But these are not the only links on this chain of gratitude. My agent, Joelle Delbourgo, is another. I can't imagine navigating the yet unfamiliar world of book publishing without her in my corner. I had a book offer in advance of having an agent, which should have been a happy problem, but to someone who likes being in control, it was a nightmare. Luckily, Joelle came to me through my life coach, Laura Berman Fortgang, the woman who helped me to redefine my life and to find the courage to take the bold steps that I write about in this book.

I met Laura through my dear friend and fellow writer Lisa Taylor Huff. Lisa is the reason I'm in Paris now. A long-time expat, she guided and encouraged me through the challenges of life in a foreign country. Together we dreamed of the day when our books would be published, but I lost my friend to cancer in July 2015 before she could achieve that dream. So, in many ways, this book is for both of us. And within its pages, Lisa can live forever, her words of encouragement continuing to inspire me and others.

I want to also acknowledge my biggest fan, i.e., my sister, Maria Anselmo, who very generously allowed me to write openly about her and our life together. We went through so much these last years and are closer for the experience. This story is as much hers as it is mine.

And to my oldest friend-cum-brother, Steven Krup, and his wife, Virginia—and all my friends who appear in this book—I thank you for sharing this journey with me and for letting me share you with the world.

This game of provenance my friend taught me, this building of a gratitude chain, is an important exercise for someone like me, who has always thought she needed to do everything on her own. But this book came into being by the grace of others. And from the process of writing this book, I have learned to let go and let others help me, allowing each to take his or her part in its outcome.

This is the ultimate lesson in humility. The more the effort is shared, the greater and more meaningful it is—for everyone. Gratitude, I've come to discover, is understanding that I am not the beginning and end, but just the little finger of a great being whose heart is in the center of the universe.